THE ABC'S OF SMALL BOAT SAILING

The authors divide mankind into three types—landlubbers, stinkpotters and sailors. Landlubbers are satisfied to remain on that one-fifth of the earth's surface not covered by water. Stinkpotters are people whose appreciation of the watered area is dulled by their noisy and fuming motors. Sailors are of two types—those who like to race and those who just like to sail. Unlike the authors of many sailing books, these authors have not won lots of sailing races, nor is that their concern in this book. They address themselves to would-be sailors from the ranks of landlubbers and stinkpotters who sense the error of their ways.

Alice Hardenbergh started sailing on her father's knee in an inland-lake Scow on Lake Minnetonka in Minnesota and later was a sailing instructor at Camp Kechuwa on the upper peninsula of Michigan. Meantime, Lincoln Clark progressed from sailing boats in his bathtub in East Cleveland, Ohio, to dinghies off Cape Elizabeth, Maine, and on Ontario's Lake Timagami. After a lapse of years pursuing degrees, she at Bryn Mawr College and the University of Minnesota and he at Wesleyan University and the University of Chicago, they married, resumed sailing, and produced a "live ballast" of four young sailors. Poor but nautically proud, they rented boats on Chesapeake Bay during wartime off-duty hours. Upon moving to Tennessee, they acquired their first jointly owned "boat"—a sailing canoe—which they "dry sailed" weekends on TVA's many lakes.

When the Clarks moved to a home on the Connecticut shore of Long Island Sound in 1952, their nautical involvement mushroomed. Following a common parental division of labor, the mother took care of the children, the father took care of the boats. What began as a hobby has become almost an obsession. He asserts that the grimness of his visage compared to that of Helen of Troy, whose face launched 1000 ships, is due to his tribulations in launching 10,000 Skimmars as President of the Connecticut Boat Company (this company merged into Aero-Nautical, Inc., in 1962 and Mr. Clark is Chairman of the Board).

Both authors are educators: Lincoln Clark as Professor of Marketing at New York University and Alice Clark in her local Parent-Teacher Association, the League of Women Voters, and the Greenwich Association for the Public Schools, which she has served as President.

THE ABC'S OF SMALL BOAT SAILING

BY

ALICE AND LINCOLN CLARK

Drawings by Barrows Peale

Photographs by Zoltan Henczel

Dolphin Books
Doubleday & Company, Inc.
Garden City, New York

The Dolphin Books edition
is the first publication of
The ABC's of Small Boat Sailing

Dolphin Books edition: 1963

To
Terry, Shepley,
Katrina, Kelsey,
and
all sailors-to-be

PREFACE

The purpose of an ABC book on small boat sailing is to tell in simple language what a would-be sailor should know. All the nautical facts of life, in the saltiest sailor's jargon, merely help to answer one basic question: "How do I safely get from where I am to where I want to be?" Left alone, a boat will go somewhere, thanks to wind, tide, and current. While an aimless ride, like a leaf upon a pond, holds a certain poetic charm, the appeal of sailing is the challenge to harness nature's forces with a piece of cloth to do your pleasure.

Books on sailing differ principally according to their concern with speed. Books for racers are typically written by experienced racers and describe their various theories on how to reach a desired destination in the minimum amount of time. The racer does not care about comfort, whether he gets wet, or whether his boat pounds or almost tips over—his goal is to beat his competitors.

This book is written of, by, and for pleasure sailors. (The racing bug may well bite you later on.) Although small boat sailing is not necessarily easier than big boat sailing, we believe that a small boat—say 8 to 18 feet—is better for a beginner. He will learn faster, since every action and every movement that he makes has a more visible and immediate effect in a small boat than in a large one. Probably the main deterrent to the joy of the sailor is the fear of what unknown pitfalls or even catastrophes his ignorance or inexperience may lead him into—from calling a "sail" a "sheet" to capsizing. It has also been our experience that often when we wanted to find out about some maneuver or term, either we were not able to find it quickly in a book, or the explanation was too abstruse and nautically worded. Hence a simply written *ABC's* with emphasis on possible pitfalls or anxieties and their solutions.

Usually a "how-to" book narrates the procedure to be followed logically step by step from the beginning—as it should—and we have followed this method in the front of our book in the *Questions of a Would-be Sailor*. Here are listed the main questions asked by beginning sailors and where to find the answers. Many people have learned to sail from a book, but down in our hearts, we believe that the first step in learning to sail is *to sail,* to go out in a boat with an experienced sailor, or to enroll in an organized sailing program. Then, when you are back home, read the *ABC's* to clarify what you have seen and done on the water.

Landlubbers often query, "Why don't sailors talk in plain English?" The answer is simply that everyday words are not as unambiguous as nautical terms. For example, the landlubber asks, "Why say *port* and *starboard* instead of left and right?" Well, *port* is always the left side of the boat, when you are *facing forward on an upright boat,* but port is not always the same as left. Port is to your right if you are facing toward the stern of an upright boat or toward the bow of an upset boat.

In order to keep the language simple and yet also let you know the correct nautical term, we have put the latter in small capitals and after the "layman's" description. However, when nautical words have become so much a part of our common language that we feel they are universally understood, we have used them without synonym or definition. "Bow," "stern," and "mast" are in this category (and, in addition, they too are to be found in their proper alphabetical places). Definition and discussion of the capitalized words are then to be found in the alphabetical arrangement. Thus the book may be used in several different ways:

Suppose you wonder what your salty friend meant as

you were returning to the mooring when he tried to explain to you about offshore winds, leeward landings, or the shoot of the boat. By glancing through the topics in the front of the book you quickly find that No. 12 is what you need, "How do I make a landing?"

Next, suppose you had pretty well gotten the general idea of the three main directions of sailing (depending on whether the wind is ahead, from the side, or from behind), but you had been a bit baffled by your friend's use of the words "beat," "close-hauled," and "close reach." Here you would want to turn directly in the alphabetical listing to the words that puzzled you and straighten out each one. Cross references are listed wherever applicable.

Now just for good measure before you go to bed, suppose you decide you had better run over some of those nautical terms again. You've done pretty well with "mast," "boom," and "jib," but when your friend got into "main halyard" and "centerboard pennant" you felt a bit confused. So turn to SAILBOAT PARTS and study the three diagrams. Then if you want verbal elaboration, look up the description under its alphabetical listing. Thus in the picture you see the word "tack" denoting a corner of the sail, but surely "tack" has another meaning—a quick glance at the T's will soon clear up the mystery.

Because of the greatly increased interest in small boat sailing in the last few years, many water-oriented communities are beginning to include sailing and water safety in their recreation programs. In this connection we would draw your attention to the entry, COMMUNITY SAILING PROGRAM.

Because of the number of variables involved, sailing remains more of an art than a science. Hence it is to be expected that any reader will find both errors of commission and omission in this book. That there are not more is due to: Thomas Hutson of the Quad Trainer Association, Pyke Johnson, Jr., of Doubleday & Company, and Stephen Richardson of the Old Greenwich Boating Association.

There would be even fewer if we had known how to accept all their kindly attempts to guide us.

Good winds and sunny weather!

Alice and Lincoln Clark

Old Greenwich, Connecticut
   January 1963

LIST OF DRAWINGS

QUESTIONS OF A WOULD-BE SAILOR
AND WHERE TO FIND THE ANSWERS

QUESTION	SEE
1. What does a sailor call the parts of his boat?	sailboat parts
2. How does a sailor state a boat's directions?	direction
3. What words does a sailor use in the act of sailing?	action words
4. What should I do before casting off?	readying
5. How do I make the boat go where I want it to go?	points of sailing
6. How do I tell where the wind is coming from?	wind
7. How do I leave a mooring or dock?	under way
8. What do I do if the wind is coming from in front of me?	beat
9. What do I do if the wind is coming from the side?	reach
10. What do I do if the wind is coming from behind me?	run
11. How do I turn around?	come about, jibe
12. How do I make a landing?	landing
13. What should I do before going ashore?	shipshape
14. How do I read the nautical "traffic signs"?	buoy
15. How do I tell who has the right of way?	right of way

1

16. What do I do if the boat tips too much? **heel**
17. What do I do if the boat tips over? **capsize**
18. What do I do if the boat goes aground? **aground**
19. What do I do if someone falls overboard? **overboard**
20. What do I do if a storm comes up? **storm**
21. What do I do if there is too much wind? **heavy weather**
22. What do I do if there is too little wind? **light air**
23. What if the boat begins to go backward? **in irons**
24. What other trouble might I run into? **distress**
25. How do I tell the various types of boats apart? **rig**
26. What is the best boat for me? **choosing a boat**
27. What accessories do I need? **gear**
28. How do I take care of my boat? **maintenance**
29. What knots do I need to know how to tie? **knot**
30. How do I organize a sailing program? **community sailing program**

A

abaft Behind; more toward the stern of the boat. See DIRECTION.

Abaft the beam is back of the middle of the boat, or toward the stern, whether on or off the boat.

abeam To the side of a boat; more exactly, off the boat at a 90° angle to the KEEL line; for example, *the wind is abeam*. See DIRECTION.

aboard On the boat.

about On the opposite TACK. See COME ABOUT.

action words Words used in the act of sailing.

Because the whole nautical vocabulary can be pretty bewildering at first, we have made some word groupings (for other such groupings, see DIRECTION and SAILBOAT PARTS), gathering together in one place terms that have something in common. In this section, we have assembled some of the words used in the actual act of sailing: what you do to or with a boat or its parts, like PINCH; or what the boat does under your guidance, like SHOOT. Each word in the following groups is defined in the body of the book.

COMMAND WORDS USED BY THE SKIPPER

cast off	ready about (or *stand by to come about*)
hard-alee	
jibe-ho	ready to jibe

THINGS A SKIPPER DOES AND WAYS IN WHICH HE SAILS

backwind (a sail)
bear off, bear away (to ~)
before the wind (to sail ~)
bend (a sail)
bring to (a boat)
by the lee (to sail ~)
by the luff (to sail ~)
cast off (a rope)
cleat (a rope)
close-hauled (to sail ~)
down (to head or sail ~)
ease (a rope)
free (to sail ~)
furl (a sail)
headway (to make ~ in a boat)
jibe (a boat or a sail)
leeway (to make ~ in a boat)
off the wind (to sail ~)
on the wind (to sail ~)

pay out (a rope)
pinch (a boat)
reef (a sail)
rig (a boat)
snub (a rope)
spill (the wind)
splice (a rope)
start (a rope)
steerageway (to make ~ in a boat)
sternway (to make ~ in a boat)
sway up, sweat up (on a rope)
trim (a sail)
unbend (a sail)
up (to head or sail ~)
whip (a rope)
wing and wing (to sail ~)

THINGS A BOAT (OR, WHEN SO NOTED, A SAIL) DOES

beat
broach to
capsize
come about
draw (sail)
fall off
foot
go about
heave to
heel
in irons (to be ~)

jibe
luff, luff up
point
reach
run
shoot
sideslip
tack
wear
yaw

aft Toward, in or near the stern of the boat, as *to go aft* is to go toward the stern. See DIRECTION.

after Back of the middle part of the boat; toward the stern, as the *afterdeck* or the *after sails*.

aground Touching the bottom so that the boat cannot move.

4

This is more serious for a KEEL boat than for a CEN-TERBOARD-type boat. In fact, in the latter you are usually warned by the sound of the centerboard scraping, or by its jumping in its TRUNK. (The same thing is true of a DAGGERBOARD except that it is not hung on a pivot and so is more likely to crack or break when it hits bottom.) Pull centerboard or daggerboard up quickly and turn back to deeper water. If you are stuck anyway, one or more or a combination of these ideas may help: (1) Push off with an oar, paddle, or any possible substitute. (2) Pull in your sails and place your weight (BALLAST) in such a way as to make the boat tip (HEEL) so as to enable you to sail off. (3) Drop your sails, place your ballast as far as possible from the "stuck" part of the boat, and push off with an oar. (4) Toss out an anchor and try to pull your boat up to it (KEDGING), although all too often the anchor is pulled to you! (5) Get out (but not in deep mud) and push, trying to lift at the same time (lift and push with your back, facing away from the boat). (6) If the bottom is mud, stay in the boat and rock it to make a sort of trough for the boat to slide out on.

Always try to turn your boat back toward where you came from, as you know you were floating then, whereas ahead it may be even more shallow. If a keel boat is stranded, consult your tide table, and if the tide is rising, wait. Otherwise, try the above methods, and especially get the boat to heel as much as possible; then the bottom of the keel, which is caught, will be freed. Or give up and get towed off by a powerboat. Best of all, watch the CHART and NAVIGATIONAL AIDS and do not get stuck at all!

air roller Inflatable canvas or rubber cylinder, used in rolling a boat in and out of the water.

alee To the side of the boat away from the wind, the LEE side. See HARD-ALEE.

aloft Above the deck; overhead.

amidships In the middle of the boat, either lengthwise or breadthwise or both. See DIRECTION.

anchor **1.** Heavy device placed on the bottom (of ocean, lake, or other body of water) to hold a boat in place, and to which it is attached by a chain or a rope (LINE) or combination of both. **2.** To secure by means of an anchor.

Anchors come in a multitude of makes and types. The kind needed for each particular spot depends on whether the bottom is sandy, muddy, or rocky. Consult experienced sailors or boat dealers in your neighborhood for advice on what is needed. The proper size (in addition to the size of the boat) depends on such factors as the harbor exposure, wind velocity, strength of current or tide, and design of the anchor. A MUSHROOM anchor is usually recommended for a permanent mooring for a small sailboat. See MOORING.

Anchoring your boat temporarily is like making a landing—you must first make your boat come to a stop —so turn your boat into the wind to make it LUFF UP. You must do this about three boat lengths above (to WINDWARD of) your chosen spot, as you will drift back in the process of anchoring.

When you have luffed up into the wind, lower the sail and drop the anchor, letting (PAYING) out the rope until the anchor touches bottom. Try to estimate how much rope has been paid out, and fasten (SNUB) the rope temporarily to a CLEAT or BITT until you are sure the anchor has taken hold on the bottom. Now pay out *at least* twice as much anchor line as has already been paid out (the SCOPE). This absolute minimum, which is about three times the depth of the water, is usually sufficient under the *most* favorable conditions. Any other type of weather, tide, current, anchor, or anchorage would mean increasing the scope up to five to seven times the depth of the water. The longer the line, the easier it is for the anchor to dig into the bottom, and

6

the safer you are. Try to have your anchorage in a sheltered spot and where the bottom is a mixture of sand and clay. When you wish to leave the anchorage, pull your boat up by the anchor rope so that it is over the anchor, hoist sail, and raise, clean, and store the anchor as you sail off.

annual variation See VARIATION.

anti-fouling Capable of preventing soiling; refers to paint or other substance which will help to prevent marine growth on the bottom of a boat riding at a MOORING all summer.

Even though you have applied such paint to your boat in the spring, you may find it turning green and scummy-looking by midsummer. This will not do any actual damage, but will slow you down, and a good scrubbing is in order. To clean off barnacles, oil, or scum, the boat may have to be turned on its side. See CAREEN.

astern Toward the stern of the boat; off the stern, or behind the boat. See DIRECTION.

athwart or **athwartships** Across the boat. See DIRECTION.

awash Water just coming over the side of a boat (occurs when a boat is HEELING).

B

back To pull a sail over into the wind on the opposite side from where it would normally be, as *to back the jib* in order to get out of IRONS. See BACKWIND.

backstay Wire or rope support running AFT from the mast to the stern of the boat to hold the mast in place.

The backstay is usually attached permanently to the stern and is therefore part of the STANDING RIGGING. However, on some boats such as Stars and inland-lake Scows, there are two backstays running to the after-deck to support the mast. Since these must be shifted each time the sail is changed from one side to the other, they are part of the RUNNING RIGGING and are called RUNNING BACKSTAYS, RUNNERS, or preventers. They are especially necessary when RUNNING BEFORE THE WIND.

backwind 1. To throw the wind from one sail onto the back side of another, as by pulling in the JIB so tightly that it backwinds the MAINSAIL and makes it flutter (LUFF). 2. To throw wind from sails of one boat onto those of another in a disturbing manner. 3. Breeze thrown on one sail or set of sails by another. 4. To hold a sail out toward the wind (to WINDWARD); to back.

Backwinding the jib can be helpful in getting away from a MOORING or when you are IN IRONS. The jib is filled with wind, the bow of the boat is blown around, the mainsail can fill, and the boat move forward. See IN IRONS.

ballast Weight in the boat to give it stability.

The crew is *live ballast* as it shifts weight in accordance with wind, weather, and direction. In TACKING, the

9

crew changes side each time the boat COMES ABOUT to give it just the right TRIM. In a heavy wind the crew must lean way out over the side (HIKE OUT); in a light wind the crew must move slowly and sit low in the boat so as not to jerk it and shake the wind out of the sails or offer wind resistance.

bare poles With all sails down.

batten **1.** To make fast and tight, as *to batten down.* **2.** Long thin strip of wood or plastic inserted in batten pockets along the outside edge (LEECH) of the sail to keep it in shape. See SAILBOAT PARTS.

JIB battens (if any) and battens in some small MAINSAILS are sewn in permanently. However, most mainsail battens (usually three or four in number and of varying lengths) are removed when the sail is not in use. They are held in pockets (which are usually about an inch larger than the batten so as not to tear or pull the sail) by snaps, or by small cords through a hole in the batten (use a SQUARE KNOT), or by an angled pocket. Have a special place to store them when you are "putting the boat to bed" and keep an extra set there for emergencies.

beam **1.** Breadth of a boat at its widest point. **2.** Point outside the boat in line with the beam (as in **1.**), and thus at right angles to the fore-and-aft line of the boat, as a vessel was sighted *on the port beam.*

beam reach A position of sailing in which the wind is at right angles to the boat (ABEAM) on one side and the sail and BOOM let out halfway, or at about a 45° angle, on the other side. See POINTS OF SAILING, REACH.

bear To be situated with respect to a compass point or the direction in which you are looking, as the lighthouse *bears north-northeast.*

bear away To go farther away from the direction from which the wind is blowing than you are now sailing; to bear off; to fall off; to go to leeward.

bear off See BEAR AWAY.

bearing Direction of an object from your boat, as used in navigating.

Bearings are given in terms of degrees (0° to 360°) or points (0–32). You *take a bearing* when you sight an object and note its compass direction. See COMPASS, POINT. A *cross bearing* is a position gotten from two or more bearings on visible objects.

beat **1.** Sailing course with the wind coming directly toward you. **2.** To sail toward the direction the wind is coming from, with sails pulled in as far as possible (CLOSE-HAULED), in zigzag fashion, first on one TACK, then on the other; to beat up; to sail into the wind; to beat to WINDWARD; to sail to windward; to sail on or by the wind; to tack; to work or to work up.

Although "beating" is sometimes used synonymously with "close-hauled," we prefer to differentiate them in the following manner: to beat (a verb) means to advance to windward or toward the direction the wind is coming from by a series of tacks; whereas close-hauled (an adjective) describes the trim of the sails when beating. We have also chosen the single word "beat" in preference to longer phrases, such as "to sail to windward," for use in conjunction with the commonly accepted single words "reach" and "run" to describe the three basic sailing directions: (1) sailing into the wind—*beating;* (2) sailing at right angles to the wind—*reaching;* and (3) sailing with the wind—*running.*

Beating is the most difficult and the most challenging, as well as the most exciting and wettest, of the three main directions in which a boat can sail. Beating is necessary when both your objective and the wind are directly in front of you. A sailboat cannot sail against the wind, i.e., point its bow directly into the direction from which the wind is coming, since there would be nothing to propel the boat—the wind would slide down both sides of the sails at once, causing them merely to flap. Therefore, the boat must zigzag (tack) so that the

11

wind will be first on one side of the sails, then on the other. See POINTS OF SAILING.

The STARBOARD TACK is a course on which the wind is from the right or starboard side of the boat and the sail is on the opposite side, or to PORT. The port tack is when the sail is on the starboard side. See TACK. Since each tack is approximately at right angles to the previous tack, beating is necessary when your objective is anywhere within this 90° arc. See Fig. 1.

In beating, your sails are pulled in tight. The end of the BOOM is approximately over the lower (LEEWARD) TRANSOM corner of the boat, and the JIB is roughly in line with the MAINSAIL.

In contrast to reaching or running—when you can pick a fixed point as an objective and sail directly toward it—in beating, although your objective is right in front, you cannot head for it directly, and your course is set by the wind itself and its fluctuations. Here your objective is to sail as close into the wind as possible and yet still keep moving along efficiently, that is, keep FOOT-ING. This is tricky, and there are two pitfalls: (1) sailing too close into the wind, called PINCHING, and therefore losing speed, or (2) sailing too far away from (OFF) the wind, and therefore losing ground (as the angle between you and your objective gets wider and wider). How can you strike a happy medium between these two extremes? Here are two suggestions: (1) Always keep your sail full. The minute it starts to flutter and soften up—to LUFF—on the edge along the mast, you know you are heading too close into the wind, that the wind has crept around to the other side of the sail. Steer the boat away from the wind (by pulling the TILLER "up," away from the sail) until the sail is full again, just to where the luffing stops, but (2) Do not go beyond that point, that is, do not sail *too far* away from the wind. Since there is no immediate visible sign to warn you (as when the sail luffs in pinching), sailing too far off the wind is harder

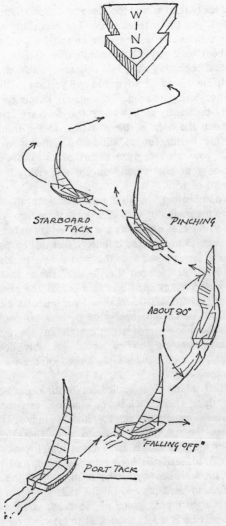

Figure 1. Beating

to identify than sailing too close to it. Sometimes, but not always, you tip or HEEL more. The best thing to do is to keep continually testing your course by gently heading the boat back toward the wind's direction until just the faintest beginning of a luff becomes visible next to the mast. Then head off a fraction and you are neither pinching nor losing ground. This means keeping your eyes pretty constantly on the LUFF (now we are using "luff" to mean the edge of the sail next to the mast), when you are beating up to windward. After you "get the feel," you can recognize a sort of sluggishness on the part of your boat when you are not giving it the right amount of wind.

When beating, the jib is pulled in tight, about parallel to the mainsail, but with this word of caution: don't pull it in so far that it deflects the wind onto the back side of the mainsail and makes it flutter. Test this by pulling the jib in as far as possible so that you see the mainsail begin to shiver, then let out the jib until the mainsail is full again, and CLEAT the jib at that point. The relative trim of the jib vis-à-vis the mainsail can also be affected by the LEAD of the jib sheet—that is, how far back on the deck the jib sheet is led through an eye fitting, the FAIRLEAD—but the novice would probably do well to accept the boat builder's placement of the jib lead for the time being.

When sailing close-hauled, or beating, the boat heels more than when reaching or running, and the skipper and crew usually sit on the high (windward) side to balance the sail on the leeward side. The skipper thus pushes the tiller down away from him ("puts the helm down") to head the boat into the wind, and pulls the tiller toward him ("puts the helm up") if the sails are not full, to head off and fill the sails.

In a light breeze, some of the crew, and perhaps the skipper if he is alone, should sit to leeward, on the same side as the sail, since in beating the boat should never heel to windward. See HEEL. Have a member of the crew responsible for watching out for "traffic" to leeward, as it is hard to see on that side in a stiff breeze. (Some sails now have a plastic window for this purpose.)

If the boat tips too much from a sudden gust of wind, water may come into the COCKPIT (you will be SHIPPING water) and you may be in danger of CAPSIZING (or fear it anyway, which is worse!). You have two remedies to make the boat come "back onto its feet":

(1) Let out the MAINSHEET until the mainsail flaps, empty of wind, or

(2) Push the tiller away from you so that the boat turns into the wind and again ends up with flapping sails; or do both at once. Be just as alert, however, to fill your sails again once the heeling is remedied, as you do not want to lose your forward motion. Remember that a RUDDER in a boat without forward motion has no effect (try pushing it back and forth at your MOORING and see). So as soon as you can, pull the sail back in (TRIM it), or pull the tiller back toward you to head the boat away from the wind (BEAR AWAY) and thus fill your sails.

When you want to shift from one tack to another, you must COME ABOUT, that is, turn the boat into the wind and beyond so that it blows on the other side of the sail and puts you on the other tack. See COME ABOUT.

Beaufort wind scale See WIND SCALE.

becalmed Without wind. See Plate 46.

becket bend Knot used for the purpose of tying two ropes together, especially ropes of different size, or fastening a rope's end to an EYE; a sheet bend.

before the wind With the wind behind and sails and BOOM out at right angles to the boat; off the wind; downwind; downhill; running free. See RUN.

belay 1. Stop, as given in an order. 2. To tie a rope to something, usually a CLEAT.

belaying pin Wood or metal pin (usually on a RAIL) to which a rope is tied.

belly See POCKET.

below Down; beneath; under.

bend 1. Knot used to fasten one rope to another or to a SPAR. 2. To tie; to make something fast; *to bend a sail* (or *bend on a sail*) is to attach it to the mast, boom, or other spars. See READYING.

Bermuda rig, Bermudian rig Triangular-sailed RIG, as opposed to a GAFF RIG; a jib-headed rig; a Marconi rig. See SAIL.

bight 1. Any part of a rope except the ends; a loop of rope bent back on itself; a bend. See KNOT. 2. Small bay or inlet.

bilge 1. Curved part of the hull which is below the waterline. 2. Inside of the hull where the water collects.

bilge board Board attached, one on each side of a boat, which serves instead of a CENTERBOARD—to retard the sideways slipping (LEEWAY), of the boat when CLOSE-HAULED; a side board.

The boards are dropped through the deck and the bilge with ropes and BLOCKS, rather than over the side on a pivoting bolt as in the case of LEEBOARDS. When sailing into the wind (BEATING), the board on the same side as the sail (the LEEWARD board) is always down and the board on the "high side" (the WINDWARD board) raised, except as needed in heavy weather. In this case, especially on the swift inland-lake Scows, the windward board is often lowered somewhat so that the crew can climb out backward over the side and use it as a platform to stand on temporarily (HIKE OUT) to help counterbalance the tipping (HEELING) of the boat.

bilge water Water that collects in the bilge.

Always bail out your boat before setting sail, but take care not to cut or mar your flooring with a metal pump or sharp-edged bailer.

16

bitt Iron or wooden post set in the deck for mooring or towing lines.

bitter end Last bit of untied rope.

blanket To cause a boat to be cut off from the wind, as by sailing to WINDWARD of it, or because of an obstruction, such as a headland.

block Grooved wheel (SHEAVE) that rotates on a pin fastened to a frame, case, or shell; on the shell are one or more hooks, eyes, or straps for attaching to an object.

A *lead block* is a convenience for changing the direction of a rope, for example, a halyard on a mast. A *purchase block,* usually in combination with other blocks, reduces the force required to move an object. Sailors delight in devising arrangements of blocks on TRAVELERS, BOOMS, or CENTERBOARDS for greater convenience and leverage.

Of the many types of blocks, possibly the most commonly used on small boats are: the fixed eye block that remains in one position; the swivel eye block that turns on its axis; and the snatch block that is open or can be opened on one side to facilitate laying in and "snatching" out a rope. See Fig. 2 and Plate 12.

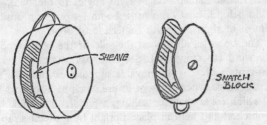

Figure 2. Block and Snatch Block

board Distance covered on a TACK when BEATING; a leg.

board boat Small (8'-12'), surfboard-like, one-sail boat. Instead of a COCKPIT, it has a flat deck over the whole HULL to sit on. Since it capsizes easily (and is easily righted), it affords a sporty and often wet ride. It usually carries a LATEEN or GUNTER rig. The Sailfish and Sunfish are popular brands of board boats. See RIG and Fig. 35.

boat hook Pole with a hook on the end to catch a MOORING.

boltrope Rope sewn along the edge of a sail. See SAILBOAT PARTS.

boom Horizontal pole (SPAR) to which the bottom of a sail (the FOOT) is fastened.

The boom is attached at a right angle to the mast either by JAWS or a hinged device called a GOOSENECK which allows it to swing in any direction. Watch out that it does not hit you on the head when TACKING, JIBING, or riding at anchor.

Since the position of the boom governs the position (TRIM) of the sail, it is important to remember the part played by the boom in the three main sailing directions: (1) wind in front, boat on a BEAT, boom CLOSE-HAULED, at its closest to centerline of boat (approximately over the back corner of the boat), (2) wind to the side, boat on a REACH, boom out about halfway (45° angle) between close-hauled and at right angles to the boat, (3) wind behind, boat on a RUN, boom let out to a position almost at right angles to centerline of boat.

The boom is always on the side of the boat opposite the wind (to LEEWARD). See SAILBOAT PARTS.

boom crutch, crotch Removable support for the outer end of the BOOM when it is not in use, such as a scissors-like X which folds up when sailing, a paddle or a stick with a notched end held in place upright by a metal strap on the COAMING.

boom vang Rope from the BOOM fastened to the HULL or COAMING close to the foot of the mast to hold the boom down when going before the wind; it can also help to prevent unwanted JIBES.

boot top Stripe painted along the waterline around the boat.

bow (pronounced "bough") Most forward part of the boat. See SAILBOAT PARTS.

bow line Rope on the bow of the boat.

bowline (pronounced "beaul'n") Knot used whenever a secure, non-slipping loop is needed. See KNOT.

bowsprit Pole extending forward beyond the bow to which to attach a sail. See RIG.

bridle Rope, chain, or wire with both ends held down, to the middle of which another rope is attached; also, sometimes, one of its parts.

On small boats, often the rope (the MAINSHEET) that controls the MAINSAIL is fastened (by a BLOCK) to the bridle across the STERN, and it is thus the same as a TRAVELER. See SAILBOAT PARTS.

bring to To stop a boat by heading it up into the wind.

broach to To swing sideways into the wind when RUNNING FREE, usually because of heavy seas.

This can be dangerous, especially if the BOOM gets caught in the water and starts to drag the sail in as well, thus weakening the RUDDER's steering power. Drop the CENTERBOARD to prevent the rolling and keep firm control of your rudder so that you can quickly counteract the boat's desire to swing into the wind; or change your course; or take a REEF.

broad before the wind With sails far out, before the wind; free; sailing downwind.

broad reach Position of sailing between a BEAM REACH and a RUN. See REACH.

bulkhead Crosswise partition below deck in the hull of a vessel that provides structural strength and sometimes divides the hull into watertight compartments.

bulwark Protective wood rail above deck to keep people and things from going overboard.

bunt Middle part of a sail; baggy part of a sail; in REEFING, the part of the sail between REEF POINTS and BOOM or between rows of reef points.

buoy Floating marker anchored to the bottom.

Buoys are of two types: (1) mooring buoys to which

boats are tied, see MOORING, and (2) navigational buoys, used as aids to navigation, to point out something specific, such as a channel or a reef. Since these buoys are the signposts and traffic markers of the water, it is important to know their meanings as described below. See Fig. 3.

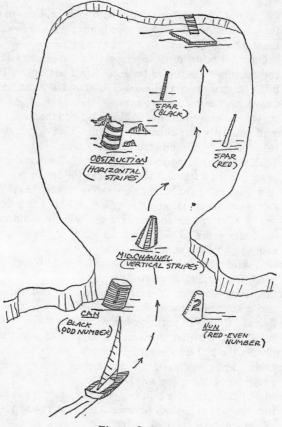

Figure 3. Buoys

TYPES OF BUOYS
(not applicable to Mississippi River)

black can buoy (also called a can) A plain black metal cylinder marked with an odd number and on your left (PORT) as you approach shore (and therefore on your right as you leave the harbor).

red nun buoy (or nun) A cone-shaped metal red cylinder with an even number and on your right (STARBOARD) as you approach shore. (Remember "red, right, returning.") The numbers on both cans and nuns go up as you approach shore.

green buoy Dredging going on.

white buoy Safe anchorage (sometimes an anchor is painted on the buoy).

white buoy with a green top Dredging or a survey.

yellow buoy Quarantine anchorage.

black-and-white vertically striped buoy The middle of the channel; keep near it.

red-and-black horizontally striped buoy Either a junction with another channel or an underwater obstruction; beware of it.

spar buoy A post. Same meaning as can or nun marking a channel, red for right and black for left when entering from seaward.

bell, gong, or whistle buoy Buoys with special sounds to mark shallow waters.

In addition to knowing markers, coastal sailors should purchase the CHARTS for their area, since these are indispensable if you venture outside your home cove. See CHART, LIGHT.

buoyage, buoyage system Succession or arrangement of buoys to serve as guides for boats.

burdened Not having the RIGHT OF WAY; opposite of PRIVILEGED.

The burdened boat is the one responsible for altering its course when it meets another boat on a collision course. See RIGHT OF WAY.

burgee Small pointed or swallow-tailed flag, usually designating boat owner or yacht club and flown from the top of the mast.

by the lee With the wind on the same side as the MAINSAIL (when RUNNING or sailing before the wind).

21

Sailing by the lee is dangerous, since it means that the wind has gotten around to the back of the sail and is just about to push it over the other side of the boat. You may JIBE accidentally any minute and hurt crew, boat, and equipment. You will be warned by the JIB's being blown over onto the opposite side from the mainsail, or a flutter in the mainsail; also, keep your eye on the TELL-TALE for a sign that the wind has shifted. To avoid sailing by the lee, head the boat a bit to WINDWARD, so that the wind comes over the side of the boat opposite from the mainsail, by pushing the TILLER toward the sail. See RUN.

by the luff With the mainsail flapping (LUFFING) somewhat, on purpose, in a strong wind. See HEAVY WEATHER.

by the wind As close into the wind as possible; close-hauled.

C

calk, caulk To force OAKUM or cotton into the seams between the planks of a boat's sides or bottom to prevent leaking.

cam cleat See CLEAT.

can, can buoy See BUOY.

canoe Long, narrow, lightweight boat, pointed at both ends, and propelled by paddles.

A sailing canoe, outfitted with a sail, LEEBOARDS over the side, and a RUDDER (all demountable), makes a convenient type of portable sailing craft, especially in a region of many lakes.

capsize 1. To place a coil of rope so that it can run freely up to its cleat. 2. To tip over; to overturn. See Plates 35–40.

Too much wind is the obvious and usual cause of a boat's tipping over so far that first the deck, then the sail and (usually) crew are in the water (see HEEL for ways to avoid capsizing). Remember, however, that an important element in avoiding capsizing is the continued forward motion of your boat. The RUDDER is the key to heading into the wind and thus counteracting HEELING, but the rudder's ability to react, to enable you to LUFF UP, is gone if there is not a stream of water flowing past it. By the same token, if you have let your sail out to spill the wind to overcome heeling, pull it in again as soon as you can, before the boat loses headway.

The novice sailor may fear the thought of capsizing. If you have this feeling, why not capsize your boat on purpose? You can pick your own time and place—a warm, sunny day and a friend nearby in a rowboat—and then that moment when the sail slowly settles down in the water will hold no terrors for you. Whether your capsizing is planned or unplanned, here is what to do: (1) Climb up to the "high" side as the boat goes over (you do not want to get the sail wrapped around you). (2) Whatever you do, don't leave the boat. (3) If you have not already got your life jacket on, put it on. (4) If you have a spare life jacket, tie it to the MASTHEAD to help prevent the boat from TURNING TURTLE. (5) Try to rescue floating GEAR, but remember it is more replaceable than you are. (6) Push down the CENTER-BOARD, if it was previously raised. (7) Try RIGHTING; some small boats nowadays with little or no COCKPIT or with effective built-in buoyancy can be righted without getting the sail down. Get all of your crew pulling on the side of the boat out of the water, with as much weight as possible on the centerboard, and then as the boat rights itself, quickly clamber over onto the other side so that as the wind catches the sail, the boat won't flop again the other way. (8) Usually, however, you must get the sails down as quickly as possible. You will be glad you have fastened (BELAYED) and coiled your HALYARDS correctly, as trying to untangle a rope while you tread water and push the heavy wet sail toward the deck at the same time is hard. (9) Now right the boat as described above (getting even more leverage if necessary by hauling on a halyard as you lean out, standing on the centerboard). (10) Start bailing. Hopefully, you have not lost your pail or pump, but you can even splash the water out by hand if necessary. If the top of the centerboard TRUNK is still under water so that it comes in as fast as you bail, stuff the opening with whatever is at hand (some boats have a piece of wood made for the purpose). (11) If all goes well, you can soon raise your sail and be on your way, but if you have any trouble, wait for a tow back to shore (always put the towrope

24

around the mast), where you and your sails can dry out
in safety and leisure.

KEEL boats seldom capsize, as the weight of the keel
pulls the boat back into position after a KNOCKDOWN.
However, a keel boat can become filled with water and
SWAMP and even sink if it is not equipped with some
sort of airtight compartment or other buoying device.

careen To tip a boat on its side, intentionally.

In order to clean or repair the bottom of a boat, it
may be careened. First run the boat onto a beach and
swing it sideways, parallel to the water's edge; then from
the water side of the boat, grasp both ends of the JIB
HALYARD (or if no jib, the MAIN HALYARD) and slowly
pull the boat over, so that the mast is in the water and
the bottom faces the shore.

carrick bend Type of knot.

carvel, carvel-built Type of HULL construction in which
the boards are placed edge to edge, thus making smooth-
surfaced sides; opposite of LAPSTREAK or CLINKER-BUILT.

cast off 1. To let go, especially in leaving a MOORING or
dock; to untie. 2. Order given by skipper to crew to untie the boat.

catamaran Sailboat with twin HULLS connected by a platform and by a bar between its two RUDDERS.

catboat One-mast, one-sail small boat.

Compared to a SLOOP, the mast is fairly far forward
on a catboat, since no JIB is carried in front of the mast.
The sail may be four-sided, usually a GAFF type, or
three-sided, usually a MARCONI type. Such rigs as LATEEN,
GUNTER, LUG, etc., are also variations of three- and four-
sided sails found on catboats. See RIG as well as name of
sail. Sailing DINGHIES are usually catboats.

Catboat fans maintain that the one-sail type of boat is
best to learn on. Because it is simpler to handle than a
boat with two sails—mainsail and jib—a beginner can
pick up the rudiments of sailing more quickly, take his

boat out alone, practice all he wants to, and become master of his own craft in short order.

Many clubs, waterfront safety programs, camps, colleges and FROSTBITE associations have adopted a cat-boat class boat for this reason. Some popular class cat-boats include: Beetle, C-boat Scow, El Toro, Interclub, Moth, Penguin, Quad (also convertible to a sloop), and the BOARD BOATS. See SLOOP.

catspaw Little wind ruffling the water; patch of water itself.

A skipper keeps an eye out for these little gusts as they can both help and hinder. If he is BEATING to WIND-WARD and not doing too well, the catspaw can give him that extra little wind he needs to make his objective or overtake his rival. On the other hand, it may blow him off his course or even capsize him if he is unwary. See HEEL, WIND.

centerboard Flat piece of wood, metal, or plastic, let down into the water under the boat, through a hole or well, covered by a framing (TRUNK) in the center of the boat. The centerboard keeps the boat from slipping sideways (MAKING LEEWAY) when sailing into or against the wind. See HULL.

The centerboard is usually pivoted on its front edge and pulled up and down the desired amount by a rope (the centerboard PENNANT) and a drum or pulley arrangement. The general rule for the position of the centerboard is: all the way down while BEATING; half-way down while REACHING; pulled up when RUNNING; with appropriate variations in between. See BEAT, REACH, RUN.

However, a beginner may well leave it down all the time. Having it down when he first comes on board will help steady his boat while he is putting (BENDING) on the sails. It does not appreciably cut down your speed or ability to move through the water and gives you more stability. This is particularly true in rough weather and rolling seas.

If the centerboard drops or gets stuck, or if the pennant breaks, try to reach it with a boat hook inside the trunk. If this is unsuccessful, try to push it up from below with a rope passed around under the boat and then tightened. (Make a big loop and start it over the bow.) You may even have to beach your boat and push from below, unless you can coax the centerboard up as you hit bottom sailing into shallow waters! See CHOOSING A BOAT, SAILBOAT PARTS.

centerboard pennant Rope used for lowering and raising the centerboard.

centerboard trunk Wooden framing in center of COCKPIT to cover centerboard when it is pulled up. See SAILBOAT PARTS.

chafing gear See LINE.

chain plate Metal strip fastened to side of the HULL to which are attached wire supports for the mast (STAYS). See SAILBOAT PARTS.

chart Sailor's map showing the shore line, landmarks, buoys, markers, lights and lighthouses, reefs, shoals, water depths, and channels.

Every skipper should carry a chart of his local waters aboard his boat. They are put out by the U. S. Coast and Geodetic Survey, Department of Commerce, Washington, D.C. and by the War Department, Corps of Engineers, U. S. Lake Survey, Detroit, Michigan, and are usually available locally for a modest price. They are revised and improved continually. For instance, new in 1962 was a handy chart "package" for Long Island Sound sailors from Throgs Neck to New Haven. Its three sections fold into a heavy protective notebook-like cover 15½″ × 8½″, containing photographs, tide tables, sources of supplies, a logarithmic speed scale, and the Beaufort scale (see WIND SCALE) as well as information on other useful publications available from the Coast and Geodetic Survey (*Small-craft Chart Series–117*). See Plate 47.

charter To rent (a boat).

chine Where the side of the boat and the bottom meet. See HULL.

chock **1.** Rounded or horned device on the edge of the deck, usually at the bow, to hold MOORING or docking ropes in place. See Fig. 4. **2.** Cradle or wedge to hold a small boat on the deck of a larger one.

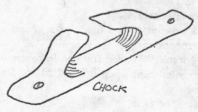

Figure 4. Chock

choosing a boat Selection of the best boat for you.

What is the "best" of all possible sailboats? Of course, the answer is that there is no such thing. There is an enormous variety of sailboats on the market which can offer you almost anything you want: speed, comfort, minimum maintenance, large capacity, small size, initial low price, safety, portability, or durability. All you can do is talk, look, listen, and then formulate your own particular requirements to help you choose the right boat for you.

One guide to help you is to find out what boats are popular in your area. Preceding generations of sailors will have taken into consideration such things as depth and nature of local waters, strength and direction of prevailing winds, etc., so that there are probably good reasons for the various types of boats found in your neighborhood.

Another piece of advice that is pretty generally applicable to a small boat buyer is to choose a ONE-DESIGN

CLASS BOAT, a boat which is built to specific measurements, like all the other boats in its particular class, to allow for the fairest competition. Even if you do not think you will ever want to race—and the chances are you *will* get "bitten by the bug," unless you are over eighty—there is always a good market for a class boat, which may not be so true for a non-class boat.

Another help in choosing is experiencing how the boat performs. Boat owners are usually glad to take you out so that you can compare several types of boats before you make your decision.

From then on you must decide for yourself. Here are some factors that you will want to consider:

(1) *Size.* Even though this book deals mostly with boats under 20 feet, that still leaves considerable leeway in choosing. If you are a young, lightweight sailor and want to go out alone, an 8–10 foot boat is a good one to learn on; for an adult beginner, 12–15 feet is probably a more comfortable size. Remember that a small boat is not necessarily the safest boat; it may capsize easily. On the other hand you do not want a boat to be too big to handle easily yourself, and this includes maintenance and spring fitting-out. In general, small boats of the size covered in this book react to wind and weather visibly and quickly, and if trouble occurs, are more easily maneuvered or repaired than larger ones.

(2) *Price, new or secondhand boats.* You can spend any amount of money for a new sailboat, even a "small" sailboat, from less than $100 for a KIT BOAT (which you must assemble yourself) to thousands of dollars for a sleek racer with several suits of sails and all the latest gear. Be sure you know what the quoted price includes—sometimes the sails are extra, or there may be a "utility" price and a "de luxe" price. Although few local dealers seem to know as much about sailboats as they do about OUTBOARDS, they are the preferable source for buying a new sailboat, because they are likely to be useful to you for servicing, storing, and trade-ins.

29

A secondhand boat can also be a good buy. If there is a well-established class in your area, you can get a used one, learn on it, see how you like it, and then sell it again. (A well-kept sailboat depreciates in value much less than a car or even a powerboat.) Just be sure to have an experienced sailor look it over before you buy.

(3) *Material*. Non-wooden boats have become increasingly popular in recent years, most of them being of fiber glass. Their appeal lies in their low maintenance— "no need to paint each spring." This is sometimes misleading since anti-fouling bottom paint is required in salt water, and after a few years fiber glass often "crazes" —develops hairline cracks—and crazed hulls have to be painted for good appearance. Also, they must have some sort of extra built-in buoyancy, are usually more difficult to repair than wood, and are usually more expensive. Moreover, fiber glass hulls vary greatly in the quality of manufacture.

On the other hand, the wood is usually uniform marine plywood with oak or mahogany framing. This combination tends to assure quality, low cost, strength, and easy repairability—but it still needs paint!

Aluminum and even steel hulls are popular hull materials in several areas. Salt-water sailors need not shun them—they are easy to treat to withstand salt water.

Coated urethane foam hulls and urethane sandwiched between two plastic hulls are recent innovations. Double hulls are neat and sound-deadening. They reduce maintenance and often increase buoyancy, stability, and hull strength. Fiber glass is still the favorite plastic in double-hull construction but others, such as "Boltaron," are gaining ground. Boltaron, since it can be vacuum-formed, assures uniform quality and permits economical production. As of 1963, however, the choice rests largely between plywood and fiber glass single hulls.

(4) *Catboat or sloop*. Whether a beginner should learn in a one-sail boat (catboat) or a two-sail boat (sloop) is again a source of much discussion. It is certainly true

that one can learn more rapidly if there are fewer pieces of equipment to handle; on the other hand, say the sloop enthusiasts, why not learn to handle a JIB from the start, since you will probably have one eventually anyway. Read the arguments under CATBOAT and SLOOP, talk to your friends, and see which is the choice for you.

(5) *Daggerboard, centerboard, or keel*. Keel boats, with a blade permanently attached to the bottom of the hull to prevent LEEWAY, are likely to be more expensive, heavier, and less versatile than daggerboard and centerboard boats, and are very uncommon among really small sailing craft. However, they are less likely to capsize and are steadier for areas where heavy winds are prevalent. Before choosing a keel boat, check the depth of the water where you would sail and moor it.

Both centerboard and daggerboard boats, on which the blade can be raised or lowered as needed, have the advantage of allowing you to sail in all depths of water, to beach your boat, and to moor it close to home in a shallow tidal cove. The daggerboard, which goes straight down through its slot, can be lifted out entirely. However, since it does not pivot up like a centerboard, it is more likely to break (something else!) or be broken if it hits bottom. There are also boats (usually cruising boats) that have a centerboard-keel combination. See HULL.

class boat   See ONE-DESIGN CLASS BOAT.

cleat   **1.** Wood or metal device usually with two arms or prongs, fastened permanently to SPARS and deck, around and to which a rope (LINE) is tied. **2.** To fasten (line) around a cleat.

Disagreement seems to exist as to how best to fasten (BELAY) a line around a cleat. Some sailors are for, some are against, circling the rope around the whole cleat; others never make a half-hitch over the prong which would have to be lifted off to be released. Certainly there is one universal rule for one particular rope on a small boat, and that is: never fasten the MAINSHEET

31

with a HALF-HITCH or any other way (since you have to be able to release it more quickly than any fastening will allow. See HEEL).

Otherwise (for HALYARDS, DOWNHAUL, etc.) try this method, which is safe and not too hard to untie: (1) Once around the bottom of the cleat. (2) Crisscross over both the top and the bottom prong to make a figure eight. (3) End by making an UNDERHAND LOOP and placing it over the top prong, so that the rope which runs out is under the loop: a locking half-hitch.

If you are worried that this is too difficult or takes too long to unfasten, here is an alternative ending, more speedily untied. Using steps (1) and (2) above, substitute for step (3) (the locking half-hitch) the following: end with an incomplete or slipped half-hitch, made by tucking a loop under the last turn around the top prong, which can be released by a mere tug. See Fig. 5.

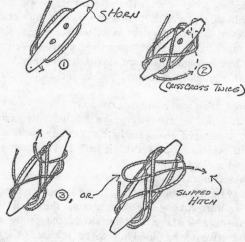

Figure 5. Fastening a Line on a Cleat

A *cam cleat* has interlocking teeth on springs (cams) instead of prongs to secure the rope. It is especially useful when speed is all-important, as on SHEETS, since a quick pull down and toward you secures the rope, and an upward jerk releases it.

A *jam cleat* is made with a V-shaped throat between the prong and its base so that when the rope is pulled tight (or "jammed"), it is held fast without need for further tying. Never put a rope *on top of* a jam cleat. See Fig. 6.

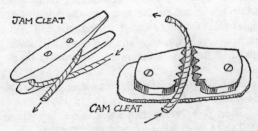

JAM CLEAT

CAM CLEAT

Figure 6. Cleats

clew Lower back (AFT) corner of a sail. See SAILBOAT PARTS.

clew outhaul See OUTHAUL.

clinker, clinker-built Type of hull construction in which the boards overlap; lapstreak; opposite of CARVEL-BUILT.

close-hauled On a course as close into the wind or toward the direction of the wind as possible; by the wind; on the wind.

In sailing close-hauled the sail and BOOM are pulled in tight (TRIMMED) so as to be over the lower edge of the COCKPIT. The boat usually tips (HEELS), and the CENTERBOARD is all the way down.

BEATING and sailing close-hauled are similar but not synonymous. Beating is sailing toward a destination directly in the direction of the wind by means of a series of zigzags (TACKS). Sailing close-hauled is the way in which you achieve this aim. To put it another way, you are always close-hauled when you are beating, but you are not necessarily always beating when you are sailing on a close-hauled course. In the latter case your destination does not require tacking; it is not directly into the wind but on a course about 45° away from the wind. See BEAT.

close reach Position of sailing between CLOSE-HAULED and a BEAM REACH, in which the boat is farther away from (OFF) the wind than when sailing into the wind or BEATING, but not as far as when the wind is at right angles to the boat (a beam reach); the sail and BOOM are just outside the boat and the CENTERBOARD is down almost all the way; a fine reach. See POINTS OF SAILING, REACH.

clove hitch Two underhand loops dropped over a post. See KNOT.

club Short pole (SPAR) like a BOOM on the bottom of a small three-sided sail, such as a JIB or STAYSAIL.

A jib with such a spar is a *club-footed jib,* in contrast to most small boat jibs, which are LOOSE-FOOTED, that is, with no boom or other wood attached.

coaming Raised edge or railing enclosing a COCKPIT or HATCH, to keep out water. See SAILBOAT PARTS.

cockpit Well or open space in the center and rear of small boats where the TILLER is located and where the crew usually sits. See SAILBOAT PARTS.

cockpit cover Cloth cover fitted to COAMING, decks, and mast to keep out the rain when the boat is not in use.

collision Coming together of two boats; two boats bumping into each other.

There is little excuse for such an avoidable mishap as a collision on the water. If you do not assume knowledge of the right-of-way rules on anyone's part (see RIGHT OF WAY) and keep out of the way of the other fellow, you should be able to go through your pleasure-sailing life free of this type of accident. (Racing is another story, when every inch and minute count, and when a knowledge of the rules of right of way is part of the game.)

Always keep a lookout for other boats (especially when you are BEATING UP with the sail pulled in and cannot see what is to LEEWARD of you), or have a member of your crew delegated to do so. This may be difficult in a heavy wind when every one is concentrating on getting up to WINDWARD (HIKING OUT) as well as sailing the boat, but it is essential.

One note of caution here on avoidance of collisions: if you are assuming ignorance of the RULES OF THE ROAD on the part of the other fellow, take your avoiding action well away from him. If you wait until you are close and it turns out that he *does* know the Rules of the Road and takes the correct avoiding action, both of you may end up doing the same thing at once—and collide!

If a collision does occur, be sure every one on both boats is accounted for and unhurt and provided with a life preserver or cushion. Then assess the damage and see whether it is possible for both boats to get to shore unaided. In accordance with the written and unwritten law of the sea, each skipper should give every and any aid necessary to the other. When there is damage to property or persons, the Coast Guard and your insurance agent should be notified.

come about To change a boat's direction by turning the boat into the wind, so that the wind comes on the other side of the sails; to go from one TACK to the other (i.e., from the PORT to the STARBOARD tack or vice versa); to tack; to go about; to make a 90° arc; the opposite of JIBE (when the wind crosses the stern of the boat, rather than the bow).

Coming about must be practiced many times by the beginning sailor until it becomes one continuous smooth action, losing as little time and forward motion as possible.

This is what will happen: you are BEATING and as skipper will be sitting on the high (WINDWARD) side away from the sail. You will push the TILLER away from you toward the sail, to head the boat up into the wind, so that it will cross through the center (the eye) of the wind. The BOOM will swing into the middle of the boat, the sail will flap as the wind slides down both sides of it at once; then, as the boat continues to turn, the sail will cross over and fill with wind on the other side. See Fig. 7 and Plate 33.

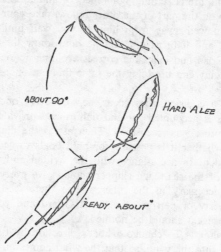

ABOUT 90°

HARD A LEE

"READY ABOUT"

Figure 7. Coming About

Now, this is what you and your crew will do: (1) Prepare your crew with the words "Ready about." (2) Then, as you actually push the tiller to the LEE side, give the order, "Hard-alee!" (3) Have one of the crew check to see if the way is clear. (4) The crew loosens the rope that controls the jib (LEEWARD JIB SHEET), letting go of it just as the boom swings over (watch your heads!). (5) The running BACKSTAY (if there is one) is loosened. (6) You and the crew change to the opposite side of the boat. See Plate 34. (7) The other jib sheet (which now becomes the leeward one) is TRIMMED and CLEATED, as is the backstay. (8) The trim of the mainsail is checked (this need not be changed since you are still sailing CLOSE-HAULED). (9) As skipper you will have brought the tiller back into the center of the boat (AMIDSHIPS), since you do not want to make a circle, but merely go at right angles to your previous position. (10) Now be sure the boat is going along well (FOOTING) with sails full, yet heading up into the wind as much as possible.

There are some pitfalls to watch out for in the process of coming about: (1) Trying to come about without sufficient forward motion (HEADWAY). (2) Not turning the boat quite far enough onto the new tack so that the sails do not fill on the other side, stopping you entirely (you may even start to go backward). Then you are IN IRONS and to get out of your predicament you must either jerk your tiller several times toward you, BACKWIND the sail, or hold the tiller over, since the RUDDER's action when you are going backward is the opposite from that when going forward. (3) On the other hand, if you come about too far and too fast, you will lose both direction and time and may even run the risk of CAPSIZING because the sails are pulled in while the boat is headed off the wind.

In coming about from a REACH, first pull in your sails and head your boat toward the wind in a tacking or close-hauled position, then come about, rather than try to go the full 180° from a starboard reach to a port reach all at once. Once you have come about, let out the sails gradually on the other tack as you turn from a close-hauled to a reaching position again. You will thus

37

avoid at least two dangers: (1) getting the end of the boom caught in the water and BROACHING TO, and (2) getting caught in irons from the loss of headway during such a wide arc.

In coming about from a RUN, when the sails are all the way out, the same method must be followed: first go to a reach, then a tack, then come about, pushing your boat slowly around as you trim in the sail and let it out gradually on the other side. Jibing is the other way to change your sail to the opposite side when on a run. See JIBE, TACK.

community sailing program   Town-wide program of sailing lessons.

There are several ways to learn to sail—by trial and error, by sailing with experienced sailors, by studying books on sailing, and by enrolling in an organized sailing program. A sailing program is particularly appealing to a beginning sailor before he has acquired a boat of his own, as well as to non-sailing parents who want their children to learn to sail properly and safely.

Instructional sailing programs are usually set up by existing organizations—camps, yacht clubs, youth and service organizations. Less common as yet, but of greater potential for extending the joys of sailing to the greatest number, are specially organized programs to provide low-cost instruction and to harness the latent sailing interests of a greater variety of individuals and organizations in a waterside community. These may be administered by a municipality itself or by a group of representatives of private organizations or by both.

One of the first and best community sailing programs in the country is that started in Boston in 1936 by Community Boating, Inc. It was the fortunate beneficiary of a gift from Mrs. James J. Storrow to the Commonwealth of Massachusetts. The state bought a boathouse on the Charles River and a fleet of sailboats and leased them to Community Boating, Inc. Now there are thirty boats sailed from early spring until late fall by children, teen-agers, and adults, both privately and in organized sailing classes.

The Boston program, fine as it is, does not, however, provide a feasible pattern for most communities to fol-low. Other towns need not wait for private benefactors or governmental subsidies. They can set up self-support-ing community sailing programs. A case illustration of a practical pattern is provided by the program that was launched in Norwalk, Connecticut, in 1962.

The CNCA. The Norwalk Community Sailing Pro-gram stems from the deliberations of the Conference on National Cooperation in Aquatics (CNCA). The CNCA, an association of twenty-four national organizations, conducts aquatic programs, has a membership constitu-ency, employs a professional staff, and utilizes volun-teers. Its members are: Amateur Athletic Union; Ameri-can Association for Health, Physical Education and Recreation; American Camping Association; American National Red Cross; American Public Health Associa-tion; American Recreation Society; Athletic Institute; Boy Scouts; Boys' Clubs of America; Camp Fire Girls; Girl Scouts; National Board, YWCA; National Catholic Camping Association; National Collegiate Athletic As-sociation; National Council, YMCA; National Federa-tion of State High School Athletic Associations; National Jewish Welfare Board; National Recreation Association; National Safety Council; National Social Welfare As-sembly; National Swimming Pool Institute; United States Office of Education; United States Power Squadrons; and Women's National Aquatic Forum.

The association also includes several technical aquatic consultants. Its purpose is to promote the exchange of ideas and the cooperative efforts of the member organi-zations to advance the entire field of aquatics—swimming, skin diving, water polo, lifeguard training, and boating, among others.

39

At the CNCA conference in 1958 the idea of sailing programs as a cooperative venture of the local representatives of the national organizations in the CNCA was presented. The "guinea pig" for trying out the idea was the town of Westport, Connecticut, which conducted a program for 128 youngsters in 1960. From an organizational point of view, however, the program had two deficiencies, which, seemingly favorable in the beginning, turned out later to be growth-retarding factors. The town of Westport subsidized the program at the outset by providing docking and other facilities, as well as funds to purchase one small sailboat and, as it eventually worked out, the program was administered essentially by the town's recreational staff. The effect of the town's generosity, however, weakened the enthusiasm of the individuals who brought the program into being, with the result that funds for more sailboats lost out to competing claimants for funds from the town fathers. Perhaps the program would have continued to develop if the organizational framework had more clearly provided for and publicized the size and interest of the community sailing constituency. After a review of the Westport experience, a modified second experiment was conducted in the adjacent town of Norwalk.

Three Ingredients for Success. Experience seems to indicate that a successful community sailing program has three basic ingredients. First is the existence of at least one individual who will devote a considerable amount of his leisure time to the program; second is the availability at low or no cost of a waterside location—a beach, a dock, or a float; third is the formation of a committee composed of representatives of several of the leading organizations in the community. Satisfaction of these three necessary conditions is not sufficient to guarantee a successful program, but makes solution of the remaining problems relatively easy—obtaining registrations, finding competent instructors, developing the details of the program, and financing boats and other equipment.

(1) *The Organizer*. Theoretically an organization can spring from the simultaneous decision of a group of individuals in response to a common "felt need." Experience indicates, however, that in the background (or in the foreground) there is usually one key person—an innovator, a promoter, an organizer, who mobilizes the group to action. A desirable organizer has three special characteristics. First and foremost, he is strongly motivated to give children and adults the opportunity to enjoy safe boating; second, he should be a respected member of one of the leading community organizations, preferably one that is affiliated nationally with the CNCA; and third, he is the kind of person who is interested in seeing that new ideas to start and improve sailing programs are inaugurated and put into effect by the community sailing committee. An example of the effective organizer is Tom Hutson, who got the Norwalk sailing committee rolling. For many years his hobby has been promoting boating-safety education, particularly for children. He preaches, "Don't cuss teenagers, educate pre-teenagers." As Commander of the nearby Saugatuck Power Squadron his standing in the community is high. Although self-effacing in that he would not accept an office in the Norwalk Committee structure, he has attended meetings regularly and has been its constant inspiration, and needle.

(2) *Facilities*. Waterfront facilities are of paramount importance to the program. It would probably be difficult to get a group of leading citizens to serve on a community sailing committee without being fairly sure that the required waterfront area would be available. Ideally the waterfront is on a body of water protected from storms and heavy seas and away from a shipping lane or harbor channel. Also ideally there is a dock or series of floats with mooring space for half a dozen boats that could be expanded as the program grew. And

41

also, ideally, there is a shed for holding classes on rainy days, to store gear and boats between seasons. But it is possible to operate with much less than the ideal set-up. Some communities may be fortunate in having someone offer the use of a waterfront location for a community sailing program, but more likely one must be found. There are several possible sources—a public beach, a town dock, a local yacht club, some individual's private property, a public-spirited marina operator. Mr. Hutson approached Louis Gardella, who owns a large marina full of hundreds of large powerboats and yachts. After hearing about the prospective program, Mr. Gardella gratuitously offered the use of one of his docks for a period of ten weeks in the summer. With this fine offer as a lever, Mr. Hutson proceeded quickly to organize the Norwalk Small Craft Safety Training Committee, which conducted the sailing program.

(3) *Sailing Committee*. The question is often raised: Why bother with a committee? An individual might conceivably be able to organize a program more efficiently than a committee. A special value of a committee, however, is that it can more quickly win public support and attention for the program. Moreover, the role of a community sailing committee is to mobilize existing but scattered community resources—it enables the community organizations to accomplish more than they could accomplish separately.

The first step in organizing a sailing committee is to invite potentially interested community organizations to send representatives to a meeting. They include the YMCA, Power Squadron, Boy Scouts, Coast Guard Auxiliary, Red Cross, and other organizations affiliated with the CNCA. The invitation to the meeting should clearly state its purpose: for example, to discuss the possible benefits of a united effort by community organizations to teach safe boating, particularly to children, and to ascertain whether there is interest in forming a committee to establish such a program. Preferably the invitations are extended first orally and then followed up with a written call to the meeting. While the organizer may extend the invitations, someone else should serve as chairman at the initial meeting. The latter will introduce and call on the organizer. During the meeting the chairman will ascertain the consensus of those present and may propose that the various views expressed be reported back to the represented organizations and that each be asked to designate a member on the prospective community sailing committee.

Organization Details. After this first meeting, the organizer writes up brief "minutes" and mails them to the several community organizations, announcing the date of the next, the organization meeting, and formally asking the organizations to designate members.

The first order of business at the organization meeting is to elect the committee's officers—chairman, vice chairman, treasurer, and secretary. The wise organizer, wishing to encourage the development of the interest of others, avoids letting himself be chosen as chairman. If it appears that he should accept some committee office, he can probably be most useful as secretary. The importance of the role of a committee secretary is often not fully realized. He has considerable power to influence the committee's actions by reviewing decisions reached at previous meetings and proposing the agenda for the next meeting.

The creation of additional committee positions should be deferred until the needs become clear-cut. For several meetings everyone should participate in every decision. Then a "division of labor" through subcommittees may be in order.

This is how it happened in Norwalk. Initial approaches to organizations were made in November 1961. Invitations were extended to them in February to attend a meeting at the local YMCA. Subsequently, the Boy

Scouts, Coast Guard Auxiliary, Mariners, Power Squadron, Red Cross, and YMCA appointed members of their organizations to serve on the sailing committee, which elected four officers. The committee held meetings almost every Wednesday night for a few months, then on alternate Wednesdays. During the following year some additional members were added, including one from a new community organization—the parents of the children in the first summer's program.

Program. After it has formed its organizational structure, the task of the sailing committee is to design its program. A concrete way to focus attention on this task is to seek decisions on what should be contained in a publicity release, a printed announcement, and registration blank for the sailing program. This involves the committee's answers to the questions: Who? When? Where? How? How Much?

Who? The "who" problem involves who will be enrolled. Many sailing programs concentrate their initial efforts on attracting children, particularly pre-teenagers. While this emphasis has the virtue of serving a group that needs instruction, it may be too restrictive. Many other age groups want to learn to sail, and why not, if they do not create overwhelming additional operational problems. A sailing committee is confronted with a constant dilemma: the greater the utilization of facilities and boats, the easier it is to cover operating costs, but the harder it is to administer the program. A committee should aim eventually, if not initially, at having programs for everyone in the community who is interested in learning to sail. For example, mothers who would otherwise be merely chauffeurs are worthy registrants. Special evening and weekend courses appeal to breadwinning fathers. Off-season programs may attract a surprisingly large number of avid "frostbiters." It is also desirable to make it possible for families to use the boats on weekends—children like to demonstrate their prowess and progress to their parents—and will they be proud!

Use of boats should be limited to those who qualify as swimmers. The committee must decide whether it will permit parents to take out boats with smaller-fry children who cannot swim, even if they are wearing life preservers. Local water and weather conditions, and insurance coverage, will help dictate the sensible policy. A reasonable requirement for children is that they hold a Beginner's Certificate in Swimming of the American Red Cross or the YMCA. For applicants to the program who do not have such a certificate, the committee may have to arrange for a test. (A common test is to require the applicant to jump into deep water with his clothes on, swim thirty feet, turn around, and swim back.) For adults it may be sufficient to sign a statement to this effect: "I certify that I can swim seventy-five yards."

It is also a prudent rule that there must be at least one qualified helmsman in any boat that is taken out at any time other than during a course. Thus if the committee plans to lease boats evenings or weekends, it should provide for a test of helmsmanship. (A stringent safety policy is essential to the obtaining of adequate insurance coverage.)

When? The "when" problem means working out the best time schedule for the program—duration of class, starting time, number of classes per week, and how many classes per session.

Interest is better sustained in a children's program that schedules five two-hour sessions a week for, say, two weeks than in one or two days a week for five weeks. Conversely, the latter schedule is better for adults. It also seems to be quite well established that the minimum course has at least twenty hours of class time. A minimum of two hours is needed for each class period. The length of the period depends primarily on how much time is needed to get the boats ready and "out to sea."

45

How many periods to schedule each day depends on the number of registrants, instructors, and boats.

As one illustration of a schedule, the Norwalk sailing committee followed a uniform schedule of four two-hour classes a day, five days a week for two weeks. The courses were repeated five times, thus consuming a total of ten weeks. Since up to three persons were registered for each boat and there were five sailboats, the capacity was sixty per term or three hundred for the summer.

Where? The "where" problem includes where to register, where to sail, where to moor, where to store gear and boats, where to meet on rainy days, where to leave messages. The real "where" problem arises from the absence of ideal facilities and requires imaginative action. For example, the Norwalk Committee, not having a place to store gear overnight, improvised by adding to a trailer a large plywood box with hinged lids. After the season, the trailer was hauled to a member's backyard. In order to improve the handling of pre-registration inquiries, the Committee intends to engage a telephone answering service. The messages it records will be followed up by the breadwinning Committee members when they get home at night. The Committee is undecided whether to have a public telephone installed at the dock—would the benefits of the service outweigh the distractions of the phone's jangling, of the paging and taking messages which would then follow?

How? The "how" question in designing a sailing program is like the grouping and teacher-utilization problem in a school. There are several ways to teach sailing, each has its advocates, and each may have its place depending on the number, knowledge, and preferences of the instructors and registrants.

In Norwalk three courses were offered: Seamanship, Basic Sailing, and Intermediate Sailing. As has been noted, each course ran two hours a day, five days a week for two weeks; the first two courses were prerequisites to the third. The chief instructor personally conducted all three courses, usually from an outboard motorboat. Several tuition-free Mariners (Girl Scouts) and Sea Scouts (Boy Scouts) designated as assistant instructors were allocated among the boats. In the final evaluation there was a consensus that while this system assured an adequate number of lifeguards, it did not fully capitalize on the abilities of the assistant instructors as teachers.

Three possible teaching approaches are summarized below: (1) The simplest system is to assign a small group of pupils to one instructor who teaches them all he can within the time available in a series of lessons that he develops. Different courses may be set up for pre-teenagers, teenagers, young adults, and parents. This system is appropriate when all the registrants are roughly the same age and are starting with the same knowledge of sailing, and when the number does not exceed two or three boatloads, e.g., six to nine pupils per instructor. The main drawbacks to this approach are the difficulties of getting competent instructors for additional groups, the possible wide variations in sailing knowledge and level of understanding, and the lack of opportunity for the faster learners to move ahead, since the pace must be geared to the slowest learner. (2) A second approach is to set up a series of courses into which the registrants are placed according to their respective sailing abilities. Five typical courses are: Seamanship (including boating safety, rowing, sculling, bending on sails); Outboard Motoring (operation and care of a motor, steering, landing, rules of the road); and three Sailing courses—basic, intermediate, and advanced. The age of the registrant can be ignored when making placements in the classes. One instructor can handle up to sixty pupils, for example, in four two-hour classes. One of the drawbacks to this method is that it is difficult to obtain the right number of registrants for each class—some classes will be too large and others too small. (3) A third approach is to break down the subject matter into several component parts so that each instructor teaches only one small segment, pupils are promoted as soon as they master each phase, and teachers are assigned as needs and numbers require. This system of instruction, widely used in teaching snow skiing, is also applicable to sailing. Here again pupils are grouped without regard to age. The assistant instructors are assigned to concentrate on teaching only one or two elements of the total program —for example, each of the following would be a different class: rowing, sculling, lectures on land, knots and rope care, bending sails, leaving a dock, reaching, running, beating, coming about, jibing, turning a mark, getting out of irons, making a landing, and capsizing on purpose. The head instructor makes the assignment of the registrants to the appropriate section, and the assistant instructor, with the approval of the head instructor, promotes the pupil to another section as soon as appropriate, whether it is after an hour or a week in the same section. Not only does this system provide a stimulus to learn quickly, but it also has several administrative advantages. It reduces disciplinary problems that sometimes arise when students do not have the challenge of enough to learn. Its "division of labor" permits utilization of willing but relatively inexperienced instructors, since they can quickly learn to teach one or two circumscribed parts of the whole. It is more flexible than other methods since the chief instructor can quickly balance his assistants with the number and ability of the registrants. Possibly its greatest appeal is the change it affords young sailors from the "lock-step" system that they usually experience in their schools.

Although several national organizations have accepted one instructor for every fifteen pupils (three in each boat) as a minimum standard, we think this is too many pupils for effective instruction, under most circumstances. This third approach is a practical way to reduce the pupil-teacher ratio since it permits the use of relatively inexperienced assistant instructors, who are easy (and inexpensive) to recruit, for limited teaching roles.

Races. There are two schools of thought as to whether or not racing should be incorporated in sailing programs. Some instructors arrange early and frequent races; others feel that premature racing, before the fundamentals are well learned, develops bad habits. Perhaps the answer is to compromise and to use races as a reward for attaining certain levels of skill, and to limit them to special days. Four bits of advice on races are: (1) Keep the courses small—the legs need not be more than twenty boat lengths; (2) Have the students choose their own race committee to organize races; (3) Have the racers organize their own protest committee to adjudicate disputes on the basis of the rules of the North American Yacht Racing Union, see RACING RULES; and (4) Stipulate that the instructor may overrule the protest committee, or even disqualify a winning boat, for poor seamanship or sportsmanship, or lack of courtesy.

How Much? The "how much" question involves two related questions: financing and fees.

While registration fees can provide sufficient income to maintain an on-going sailing program, as well as amortize purchase of equipment, a committee has an initial financial hurdle to overcome. It must acquire boats and equipment before the program starts and then arrange for payment, probably over a period of years. Although no community is *average*, an average budget might anticipate income of $2000, of which about half is required for operating expenses (salaries, insurance, publicity, gasoline, extra oars, paint, brushes, extra life jackets, etc.) and the other half for boats and equipment which can be used for several years. This sum would cover the cost of five or six small sailboats (but large enough for three teenagers), which the budget could amortize over three or four years.

The problem then becomes how to get the money needed in advance of the collection of the fees. The simplest, but not necessarily the easiest, method is for committee members or the organizations they represent to loan part or all of the needed funds. Another obvious source for loans is a local bank—traditionally banks have been rather reluctant to make marine loans, although many are now changing. Another approach is to enter into a lease-purchase agreement in cooperation with a boat manufacturer and an equipment leasing company. (This is what the Norwalk Sailing Committee did.)

Of course, it is even more pleasant to solve the financing problem by circumventing it, that is, by obtaining gifts and loans of facilities, boats and equipment from individuals, organizations, local merchants, or others.

The amount to charge as a registration fee for a course will be largely governed by the expenses which have to be covered. The fees for an adequate program need not be excessive—50¢ to $1.00 per hour is sufficient.

The Norwalk Committee just broke even in the first year of its operations, charging $10 for its twenty-hour Seamanship courses and $15 for its twenty-hour Sailing courses (with the cost of its five boats being amortized over three years). In order to add more equipment, to reimburse assistant instructors, and to provide for a few more scholarships, the Committee is thinking of raising its fees for advanced instruction next year.

The question of scholarships is worthy of special note in a community sailing program. The Norwalk Committee, for example, received contributions from individuals as well as organizations, which enabled them to enroll some children who otherwise would not have been able to participate.

Instructors and Instruction. The ideal instructor is an

expert sailor, teacher, and educational administrator. The two main sources of instructors are college students during their summer vacation, and teachers. Which is the better source cannot be answered abstractly—it depends on the availability and characteristics of the particular individuals.

The instructor has five main tasks: (1) To work out the details of the instructional schedule in accordance with the policies of the sailing committee; (2) To interview, train, and assign duties to assistant instructors; (3) To assign each registrant to the appropriate class; (4) To maintain the boats and equipment, and (5) To establish and enforce rules.

Importance of Rules and Safety. Safety is of paramount importance, and must be emphasized over and over again. Experienced instructors invariably also cite the importance of strict discipline, not only for safety but also for the protection of boats and other equipment. Safety rules include: wearing life jackets; wearing rubber-soled shoes; no running on the dock or in the dock area; following the specified course, usually in single file; no racing unless specifically authorized; no JIBING unless "jibe-ho" orders have been issued; no standing on the bow or thwarts of the boats; tying up boats to the dock with approved knots; removing oars, paddles and other equipment from the boats at the end of the class period.

A special note on life jackets—*everyone* should wear them, especially the instructors and all adults. A rule that exempts adults is psychologically undesirable; it seems unfair to children. Unless a uniform rule is enforced there is likely to be a constant unpleasant discipline problem about the wearing of life jackets.

Instructional Aids. A necessary and sizable piece of equipment which must not be overlooked when setting up a sailing program is a motorboat. Not only does the instructor use this for overseeing sailing students and as-

51

sistants, but it is also a must from the point of view of safety. In it should be an anchor, extra lines, and extra life jackets.

Unless there are permanent buoys or other objects to use as direction guides, one or more sets of portable markers is almost a teaching necessity. Two simple types are a neoprene balloon and a flag on a weighted bamboo pole, either one being attached to a small anchor. The markers restrict the teaching area (allowing the teacher to call instructions from a dock or centrally located boat), make possible drill in coming about, jibing, and making a landing, as well as marking triangular or wind-ward-leeward practice courses. See COURSE.

In addition, there is a host of useful teaching aids, both for land and water instruction: model boats, electric fan for wind, blackboard, movies, notebooks, sailing books, whistle, megaphone, as well as guest speakers and conducted visits to a boat yard or sailmaker.

Rainy days especially are a time when lectures and theory talks can make good use of the above instructional materials.

A system of simple awards and some social get-togethers will advance the whole program.

Persons who are contemplating the organization of a community sailing program may wish to write for information to the Conference for National Cooperation in Aquatics, 1201 Sixteenth Street NW, Washington 6, D.C.

compass Instrument for determining direction on the surface of the earth by means of a freely swinging magnetic needle which points to the magnetic north.

The COMPASS CARD is the most visible part of the compass's structure. It is the round card marked with all the *points of the compass* (North, North-northeast, etc.—32 in all) by which one *reads the compass* and gets one's direction. On it are also marked the degrees, starting with 0°, North; then 90°, East; 180°, South; 270°,

West, and going around the full circle of 360°. Because there are 32 points, each point is $\frac{1}{32}$ of the circle, or 11¼ degrees.

The compass floats in a sealed bowl mounted on "gimbals" so that it can remain level even when the boat tips. The LUBBER LINE is a marking on the bowl parallel to the boat's KEEL, and to steer by the compass you maneuver your boat so that the direction you want on the compass card is lined up with the lubber line; thus, if the point marked S.E. is on a line with the lubber line, then you are going in a southeasterly direction.

But wait! It is not quite so simple as that, because there are two Norths, true north and magnetic north. The compass's magnetic needle makes the compass point to the magnetic north, above Hudson Bay, Canada, whereas true north is at the North Pole, about one thousand miles beyond. Therefore, you must allow for this VARIATION by correcting your compass reading each time.

This is where your CHART comes in for it always has a COMPASS ROSE printed on it showing both true and magnetic north. The amount of variation is different depending on where you are on the earth's surface; and the inner circle on the compass rose is the magnetic compass (the variation from true north) for that particular location, and the writing at the very center spells it out in words, "Var. 14° 15 W" and the year. This simplifies greatly the conversion between true and magnetic north.

One other variation in your compass reading, called DEVIATION (in contrast to the variation from true north), must also be taken into account. Deviation is a result of magnetic influence—anything made of iron or steel—in the boat itself and must be determined for various headings for each boat when the compass is installed. While variation remains constant on any heading of the boat, deviation varies from one heading to another.

Now, why a compass anyway, and when do you need to use it? A compass, of course, performs a vital function if you are caught in a heavy fog, pouring rain, or are out on a pitch dark night. But even more than that, although there are small boat sailors who may never want to venture farther than their own home cove, for others there will come a day when distant waters beckon, and a sail to an unknown place, even an overnight trip, is the thing you want to try next. For this you want to be able to: (1) Decide the direction in which you want to go to reach your destination (your course) and follow it by the compass. (2) Decide at any given moment where you are so that you will know if you are on course (this is called "taking a fix").

To determine your course, find on your chart a buoy near home—your departure point—and another marker on the chart about 5–10 miles away—your goal—and draw a line between the two. Now with your COURSE PROTRACTOR (or parallel rulers) transfer the course line to the center of the nearest compass rose (there are usually three or four on each chart). The direction (NNE, for instance) of your course line on the inner circle, which is the magnetic compass rose, is your magnetic compass course. Thus, with the help of the rose, you have converted the true course to the magnetic course. Now, correct for deviation (add or subtract the number of degrees necessary) and you have the course to follow on your compass to attain your goal.

Suppose you have now been sailing for quite a while and you want to check your course to see how far along you are. You must take a *fix*. This may be done in various ways, by: (1) cross bearings; (2) three-way bearings; or (3) a range and a bearing.

To take a cross bearing, you must be able to see two objects (a buoy, and a steeple on the shore, for example) that are not too close together (try for a 90° difference between them). Sight the direction of one of the objects on your compass, say 005 degrees, convert to the true bearing, say 020 degrees, and then draw a line on your chart through the object at the angle you have arrived at. Your boat is somewhere on this line. By doing the same thing with the other object, you draw a second line which crosses the first, and this is where you are (or were when you began your calculations!). Because this all can be very complicated until you have actually done it, practice it beforehand until you become familiar with your equipment and procedure.

A three-way bearing is even more accurate, in that a third sightable object is used and three lines are drawn; where they cross is your boat's position.

When two objects line up one behind the other—say a church steeple is in line with a water tank, as seen from where you are, they are *in range*. Now find another object (take another bearing) somewhere near right angles to your range, and your fix is where the range line crosses the bearing line.

compass card   Circular card on which the compass needle spins, marked with the 32 points of the compass and the 360 degrees of the circle. See COMPASS.

compass point   One 32nd part of a circle; 11¼ degrees. See COMPASS.

compass rose   Set of two circles, each marked with compass degrees, printed on CHARTS to aid in piloting and navigation.

The outer circle gives the true north and the inner its related magnetic north for the area shown in the chart; the actual number of degrees of variation of this magnetic north is printed in the very middle of the rose. See COMPASS and Plate 47.

course   **1.** Direction in which a vessel is sailing. **2.** Specific path for a boat to follow, as in a race.

Since the key to sailing is making your boat go where you want it to go when the wind is (1) coming from in front of you, (2) from the side, or (3) from behind,

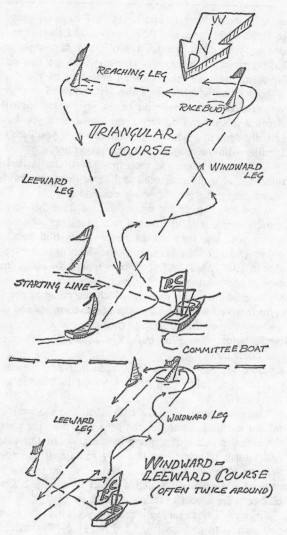

Figure 8. Racing Courses

you will have demonstrated your ability to sail when you can successfully handle these three conditions by (1) BEATING, (2) REACHING, and (3) RUNNING.

That is why most series of races are sailed over triangular and windward-leeward courses; the triangle usually means a beat and two reaches (or a beat, a reach, and a run), and the windward-leeward course, a beat and a run. Both COMING ABOUT and JIBING are also included. The America's Cup races are conducted alternatively over these two types of courses. See Fig. 8.

Each side of the course is called a LEG and markers of some sort—buoys, flags, or small boats—are used to denote the corners and the start and finish line.

Such courses are a good way for sailing classes to learn and practice all the rudiments of sailing. Even an adult teaching himself to sail "by the book" can make good use of them. You will learn how to sight over your shoulder to try to gauge whether or not you can make the buoy on the next TACK, how close you can come to the mark in both coming about and jibing, how to PINCH to make a mark if necessary—all things which will stand you in good stead even if you never go in for racing. See Plate 29.

course protractor Device for determining a boat's course on a CHART.

The course protractor, like the parallel rulers, is the means by which the navigator determines the course which he will follow on his compass.

It consists of a celluloid disc marked with the compass points and degrees and a movable straight edge pivoted from the center of the disc.

cow's-tail Frayed rope end; Irish pennant.

crank, cranky Inclined to tip (HEEL) too easily; tender.

crew 1. Person or persons who help the skipper sail the boat. 2. To help the skipper sail the boat.

A good crewman is an important asset to any skipper (especially, of course, in racing). He keeps his skipper informed on the location of other boats, buoys, etc.; he knows just what is expected of him when GOING ABOUT, JIBING, making a landing, and other maneuvers, and can often anticipate the skipper's request to HIKE OUT, change the position of the CENTERBOARD, etc. He can suggest a course of action, but not argue it, and always abides by the skipper's decisions.

cringle Eyelet set in a sail for tying purposes, usually in the corners of the sail, the TACK, CLEW, or HEAD. See Fig. 34.

cross bearing See BEARING, COMPASS.

crotch See BOOM CRUTCH.

crown Bottom part of an anchor where the lateral arms join the long mainstem (SHANK).

cruising Sailing away from a land base for several nights.

cuddy Small cabin or roof-covering over the front part of the COCKPIT.

current Regular movement or flow of water, either in oceans or rivers.

Ocean currents are caused by the rise and fall of the tide in and out of bays and inlets along the coast. Tidal current tables are prepared by the Coast and Geodetic Survey of the Department of Commerce, as are tide tables. See TIDE.

cutter **1.** SLOOP-type sailboat with one mast, MAINSAIL, and usually two headsails in front of the mast. The cutter thus differs from the sloop in having more than the one sail (JIB) in addition to the mainsail; it may also have a BOWSPRIT, is narrow of beam, and its mast is usually nearer the center of the boat than that of the sloop. See RIG. **2.** Coast Guard powerboat.

D

Dacron   See SYNTHETICS.

daggerboard   Removable centerboard on a small boat, to prevent sideways slipping when sailing to WINDWARD. See Plate 9.

The daggerboard is pulled up and down vertically by hand, instead of being pivoted like a centerboard. See CENTERBOARD, CHOOSING A BOAT.

day sailer   Pleasure sailboat without sleeping quarters.

dead before the wind   With the wind directly behind the boat, and the MAINSAIL and BOOM all the way out at right angles to the mast.

dead reckoning   Calculation of a boat's position on a CHART, such as the course sailed and the distance covered, from records rather than by observation of external objects.

dead rise   Amount that the bottom of a boat rises from the lowest point to where it joins the sides. See HULL.

deck   Platform which partially covers the upper part of the HULL.

On small boats the deck may be limited to a space at the bow, the stern and a narrow strip around the COCKPIT; or there may be none at all, as is usual in sailing DINGHIES.

development boat   Class boat which allows for development and change, rather than adhering to exactly the same specifications year after year; the Moth, the International 14, and the Suicide are examples of development boats. See ONE-DESIGN CLASS BOAT.

deviation Compass error resulting from magnetic action of nearby iron or steel on the boat.

The amount of deviation must be determined separately for each boat, and varies from one heading to another. See COMPASS.

dinghy Small open boat used for rowing, sailing, fishing and all utility purposes—often nicknamed a "dink."

Step in the middle of your dinghy and don't leave one foot on the dock and one in the dinghy—you may land in the water. See Plates 2–5. Don't try to step in or out of the dinghy when holding a heavy load. Get in first and then have someone hand it to you, or toss it in first, if you are alone.

Your dinghy is the faithful ferry boat to take you to and from your sailboat at its MOORING. Always approach your sailboat from the stern, so that the wind or tide will not cause you to bump into it. Fasten the dinghy by its rope, the PAINTER, to a CLEAT on the stern of the sailboat while you are getting ready to sail.

direction Point or line toward which something is aiming.

In Fig. 9, starting from AMIDSHIPS, the front half is

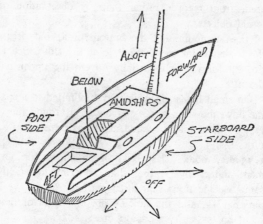

Figure 9. Direction (Standing in boat)

FORWARD, the rear half is AFT. The left side is PORT (formerly it was called LARBOARD), and the right side is STARBOARD. ALOFT is up, BELOW is down, OFF is anywhere to seaward or outside the boat.

Directions of objects *outside* the boat are given in relation to the course of the boat. These are called BEARINGS. Fig. 10 describes a circle around the boat divided into eight sectors.

Figure 10. Direction (Bearings)

Directly in front of and behind the boat are *dead ahead* and *astern*. Sideways is *on the starboard* (or *port*) *beam*. Objects exactly four POINTS from the beam are *broad on the starboard* (or *port*) *bow* and *broad on the starboard* (or *port*) *quarter*. Directions within a sector of 45° on each side ahead of the beam are *forward of the beam*, and behind the beam they are *abaft the beam*. Within the two foremost 45° sectors on each side of the bow, objects are *on the bow*; and in the two rear sectors, *on the quarter*. See POINT.

Directions are also stated in relation to where the wind is coming from. UP is toward the wind, and DOWN is away from it. The WEATHER or WINDWARD side of the boat is the side against which the wind blows; the LEE or LEEWARD side is the other side, the one away from the direction of the wind. The sail is always on the leeward side. See Fig. 11.

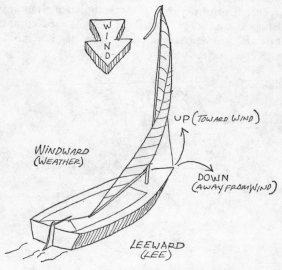

Figure 11. Direction (in relation to wind)

distress Misfortune, trouble.

The most common mishaps that can befall a small sailboat owner are listed below. Possible ways of handling such troubles are described under the word in small capital letters; otherwise, in this section.

CAPSIZED	A LEAK
CENTERBOARD stuck	Broken MAST
COLLISION with another boat	Man OVERBOARD
Lost in a FOG	Broken or lost RUDDER
Caught IN IRONS	SWAMPED

Loss or failure of any part of the boat or its equipment—through being broken, torn, or lost overboard.

Prevention of trouble in the first place is, of course, the best "cure" for any kind of distress. The careful skipper will continually be on the lookout for weak spots—a frayed piece of rope, a small hole in the sail, a loose screw or TURNBUCKLE, or other signs of wear. He will know the waters he is going to sail in, at low tide and at high tide. He will have CHARTS showing depths and obstructions in strange waters. He will keep a lookout for BUOYS, NAVIGATIONAL AIDS, and other boats. He will see that necessary equipment and provisions are on board (see GEAR), and that his passengers are chosen with regard to numbers, weight, ability, and obedience.

But mishaps occur no matter how carefully the skipper prepares. Here are some ideas for handling those not listed above: (1) If a rope (LINE) breaks, and you are unable to replace it, either SPLICE it or see if it can be shortened—perhaps by using fewer pulleys (BLOCKS). (2) If a wire STAY or SHROUD breaks, insert a rope between the two broken ends by making a loop on each. If it is the turnbuckle that gives way, do the same thing with a light line passed several times through the CHAIN PLATE on the deck and the end of the shroud. Make these repairs when the broken parts are to LEEWARD (or as you are LUFFING) so that they are slack and can be more readily pulled together. (3) If the BOOM should break, lash a pole of some sort—oar, paddle, SPINNAKER POLE—beside it and take as much strain off it as possible. (4) If a sail is torn, it should be taken down quickly, so that it will not get any worse. For a small hole, mending tape will probably hold until you get in. A SPINNAKER can sometimes be substituted for a MAINSAIL. (5) A HALYARD end inadvertently pulled out of reach while you are putting on the sails is really annoying—partly, of course, because it is an avoidable mishap. Try reaching it with the spinnaker pole and a piece of wire; or look for a high dock from which you might pull down the mast sideways sufficiently to reach the escaped rope; or send a lightweight crew member up after it (but don't capsize in the process).

distress signal Method by which a boat can draw attention to its distress.

The following methods are used by sailors in distress to call for help: (1) An S.O.S. signal, a signal using sets of threes by any available means: three dots, three dashes, three dots, with a mirror or flashlight (or of course a radio transmitter); three dips right, three dips left, with flags or other similar objects, etc. (2) A gun or loud report at regular intervals (of about a minute). (3) A continuous sounding of a fog signal. (4) A transmittal by radiotelephone of the words MAY DAY. (5) A signal consisting of a square flag and a ball above or below it (anything that resembles a ball, like a bundle of clothes, will do). (6) The International Code flags NC (the N or "No" flag is made up of blue and white checks, and the C or "Yes" flag is blue, red, and white striped). (7) A U. S. flag flown upside down. (8) A flame (from burning oil, etc.). (9) Rockets, with red stars or red lights.

Actually, most of the equipment for sending these signals is not likely to be aboard your small sailboat, and they are included here mainly in case you should see or hear another boat using them to call for help. In your case, it is probably safe to say that any amateurish shout for help, or the waving of a shirt atop a paddle, will be responded to, since the law of the sea is never to pass by a boat in distress and to help in any way you can.

ditty bag Small cloth bag on board a boat for essentials, such as pliers, extra string, scissors, mending tape.

dock **1.** Wooden platform projecting into the water from the shore at which to land a boat. **2.** To land a boat at a dock.

dory Flat-bottomed rowboat with flaring sides and deep V-shaped stern.

down   Away from the direction of the wind; to leeward.

downhaul   Rope attached to the underside of the boom where it joins the mast, and by which the LUFF of a sail is stretched tight after the sail has been raised. See SAIL-BOAT PARTS.

downhill   Same as DOWNWIND.

downwind   Away from the direction from which the wind is blowing; *to sail downwind* is to sail with the wind behind (ASTERN); before the wind.

draft, draught   Depth of water needed to float a vessel.

draw   **1.** To fill with wind (said of a sail). **2.** To be in sufficient water to float; for instance, if a boat draws three feet of water, it cannot land at a dock in two feet of water.

drogue   Canvas bag or bucket put over the side of a boat to act as a drag in heavy weather; a sea anchor.

dry rot   Decay of wood.

dry sailing   Keeping a boat out of water when not actually in use—it is hauled out after each outing and launched again at the time of sailing either by trailer or by a yacht club's lifting device. Dry sailing is practiced by finicky sailors to keep their boats clean and smooth and to prevent them from becoming waterlogged, by thrifty sailors to cut mooring charges, and by both pleasure and racing sailors who wish to sail in distant waters. See Plate 62.

E

earing Short rope to tie a sail to a SPAR; in REEFING, the line that ties the eyelet hole (CRINGLE) to the BOOM.

ease, ease off To loosen or relieve pressure; to pay out; to slack off or away; to start.

To *ease the sheet* is to let out the rope that controls a sail.

ensign National flag carried on a ship; the *U. S. ensign* is the American flag.

It is usually flown only when a boat is at anchor or when saluting while under way. At anchor it is flown at the boat's stern; under sail it is flown about one-third of the way down the outside edge (LEECH) from the top of the sail.

The *yacht ensign* is the same design as the American flag (U. S. ensign), except that instead of fifty stars, there is an anchor in a circle of stars. It is often used instead of the U. S. ensign and should be treated in the same way.

eye **1.** Loop of rope. **2.** Any kind of round hole for leading or fastening a rope, a pin, or wire, as *eyebolt*, an eye on the end of a bolt screwed to the HULL or a SPAR.

eye of the wind Exact direction from which the wind is blowing.

eye splice Loop in the end of a rope made by curving it around and SPLICING it back into its own strands. See SPLICE.

eyestrap A strip or rod, usually of metal, raised in the middle and fastened at the ends to the deck or SPARS to hold a BLOCK or guide a LINE. See Plate 19.

F

fairlead, fairleader Round metal eye or other device screwed to the deck to guide a rope in the direction desired. See Plate 19.

fairway Navigable part of a harbor, its main channels.

fake 1. Loop of rope. 2. To coil a rope in neat layers so that it will run out easily. 3. To tie up a sail by putting one fold to the right, the next to the left, and so on.

fall Part of a rope by which it is pulled. See KNOT.

fall off To head the boat away or to go away from the direction of the wind; head to LEEWARD; head away; head off.

In changing from one TACK to the other (COMING ABOUT), you should fall off on the new tack just enough to fill the sails. If you fall off too far, you will be losing ground, as your destination is toward the wind. PINCHING, on the other hand, is remedied by falling off a bit. See Fig. 1.

fast 1. Rope to fasten a boat to a dock. 2. Secure, tight (said of LINES or ropes).

Instead of "tie a rope," sailors say *"make fast a line."*

fathom Six feet.

feather To turn the blade of an oar as it is pulled out of the water so that it is horizontal while being swung back for the next stroke, in order to reduce wind resistance; the blade is rotated again to a vertical position before entering the water.

fend, fend off To keep from touching or hitting (when landing your boat at a dock) by using a boat hook, your hands or feet.

fender Any device to keep a boat from rubbing against a dock or another boat, as a cushion, a rope, a rubber tire, or kapok cylinder.

fetch To attain a specific marker to WINDWARD; to reach (your destination).

To *fetch a mooring* is to pick up or attain your MOORING buoy.

fiber glass Plastic substitute for wood, now widely used for small boats. See CHOOSING A BOAT.

figure eight knot See KNOT and Plates 10 and 20.

fill To become full of wind (said of sails).

fine reach Same as CLOSE REACH.

fisherman's bend Type of knot.

fit out To overhaul and prepare a boat for the water after a period of idleness, as over the winter.

fittings Collective name for all the devices, such as BLOCKS, CHOCKS, CLEATS, and FAIRLEADS, by which LINES, SPARS, and sails are controlled; hardware.

fix Determination of the position of a boat, obtained by taking BEARINGS.

To *take a fix* is to determine where you are by sighting and noting on your CHART the angles of two or more objects on the shore from where you are, then extending the two lines until they cross. See COMPASS.

flag Rectangular, triangular, or swallow-tailed piece of cloth of many markings and colors, important to sailors in at least three ways: (1) As identification, such as a national or a club flag. See BURGEE, ENSIGN. (2) As a method of communication. See INTERNATIONAL CODE, SEMAPHORE. (3) As a special signal, such as a storm warning or distress signal. See DISTRESS, STORM.

The three usual identification flags are: (1) The national flag (the ensign) or the yacht ensign. See ENSIGN. (2) Your yacht club's flag (the burgee). (3) The owner's flag (called the "private signal").

For regattas and national holidays, International Code flags are flown as decorations, alternating the square and the triangle. This is done only when the boat is at anchor, and the three flags listed above are never part of the display.

The owner's flag is usually a swallowtail decorated with a pattern of his own choosing and registered with *Lloyd's Register of American Yachts*.

Some other flags are: (1) Officer's flag—flown by a yacht club officer on his own boat. (2) Owner absent flag—a blue rectangle flown from the starboard SPREADER to show that the owner is not on board. (3) Guest flag—a blue rectangle with a white diagonal stripe used when guests are using the boat. It is flown under way as well as at anchor. (4) Owner's meal flag—a white rectangle flown at anchor to show that the owner would just as soon be left alone while at table.

Flags are flown from 8 A.M. until sunset. The ensign goes up first, then the burgee, and lastly the private signal; they are lowered in reverse order.

flake   Same as FAKE.

flashing light   Navigational recurring light in which the periods of darkness are longer than the periods of light. See LIGHT, OCCULTING LIGHT.

flat   Hauled all the way in, said of a sail.

flaw   Sudden short burst of wind.

float   1. Flat-bottomed platform anchored in the water. 2. Wooden raft usually attached by a gangplank to a dock or the shore in tidal waters, so that it can rise and fall with the tide.

For approaching or leaving a float in a sailboat, see LANDING. 3. Small floating object attached to the anchor rope. See MOORING.

floorboards   Wooden boards or slattings, sometimes removable, covering the bottom of a boat for protection and dryness.

fluke   1. One of the two or more pointed ends of an anchor which dig into the mud. 2. Unpredictable wind— more often *fluky*, as *a fluky breeze*.

71

fly Small pennant at the top of the mast to indicate direction of the wind; also a strip of cloth or yarn tied to the SHROUDS for the same purpose; a telltale. See WIND.

flying Not fastened or furled, as of a sail.

A SPINNAKER is *set flying* since it is not attached to MAST, BOOM, or STAY but secured only at its three corners.

flying jibe See JIBE.

fog Reduced visibility from moisture in the air.

Boats under 16 feet are not *required* to carry a foghorn but *should* in areas where there are frequent fogs. All sailors should know the FOG SIGNALS and take these necessary precautions: (1) Carry a compass. (2) Head for home if you see the fog coming. (3) Keep out of channels of heavy traffic. (4) At the first warning of fog, make sure you know where you are by some mark on the land or a BUOY (that is, take a FIX. See BEARING). (5) Then feel your way by short TACKS, or from buoy to buoy, rather than by one long markerless course. (6) If you do not have a compass, guide yourself by the wind, as its direction usually remains constant in a fog, and your own sense of direction may get befuddled. This guide is tricky; one sailor who tried to follow it is known to have circled an island!

fog signals This is how sailors indicate their direction in fog: if they are on the STARBOARD TACK or REACH, one long blast every minute; on the PORT tack or reach, two long blasts in quick succession every minute; BEFORE THE WIND, three blasts every minute. Boats at anchor ring a bell for five seconds every minute.

foot 1. Lower or bottom edge of a sail next to the BOOM. See SAILBOAT PARTS. 2. To travel forward briskly through the water, as *the boat is footing well*.

fore Near or at the front of the boat; often as a prefix, as in FOREMAST or FORESTAY.

fore and aft Lengthwise direction of the boat, in line with the KEEL.

A *fore-and-aft rig* refers to sails set on vertical masts instead of horizontal YARDS; not square-rigged. Almost all boats nowadays are fore-and-aft rigged.

foremast Mast nearest the bow.

forereach 1. To gain or overtake (another boat). 2. To go ahead or SHOOT while turning into the wind (GOING ABOUT).

foresail Sail in the front part of the boat.

forestay Supporting rope or wire from the mast to the bow.

On small boats the forestay, JIBSTAY, and HEADSTAY are all one and the same, whereas they might all be different on larger yachts. The forestay can be any STAY in front of the mast, the jibstay is the stay to which the jib is fastened (HANKED), and the headstay is the stay *ahead* of, or in front of, the others.

forward In or near the direction of the front of the boat; toward the bow; in front of; opposite of AFT. See DIRECTION.

foul 1. To touch another boat or a BUOY in a race, so as to be disqualified. 2. To cover or be covered (as of the bottom of a boat) with anything which impedes movement, such as seaweed or barnacles. 3. Against you or your boat's direction, as a *foul tide;* opposite of fair. 4. Tangled, as of ropes (LINES); caught; obstructed.

A *foul anchor* is one that is tangled up with a line or cable.

frame 1. Constructional skeleton of a ship. 2. Crosswise board in the HULL's skeleton to which the sides or lengthwise boards are fastened; a rib.

free 1. To untangle. 2. Not CLOSE-HAULED.

To *run free* is to RUN, or to sail before the wind with the wind behind (AFT). See RUN. To *sail free*, on the other hand, is to sail with the wind more than six compass points (see COMPASS) from DEAD AHEAD, the idea being that the wind *frees* the sail of being pulled in tight as the wind moves around more toward the side.

freeboard Height of the side of the boat above the water level to the deck.

frostbiting Fast-growing sport (begun in the 1930s) of sailboat racing in the winter, usually in sailing DINGHIES, such as the Penguin, Moth, Interclub, or Tech Dinghy.

furl To roll up and tie a sail on a SPAR or BOOM.

G

gaff Short SPAR projecting from the upper part of the mast—it supports the top part (PEAK) of a four-sided sail. See Fig. 12.

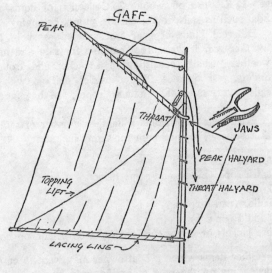

Figure 12. Gaff

gaff rig RIG consisting of a four-sided sail fastened to three SPARS: the BOOM along the bottom, the mast on the front edge, and the GAFF on the top.

There are two ropes (HALYARDS) for hoisting the sail, the THROAT halyard for the edge of the sail next to the mast, and the PEAK halyard for the top of the gaff. See Fig. 12.

gale Hard winds of 28–55 KNOTS: *moderate gale* 28–33 knots; *fresh gale,* 34–40; *strong gale,* 41–47; *whole gale,* 48–55. See WIND SCALE.

galley 1. Kitchen on a boat. 2. Ancient vessel, propelled by oars.

garboard See STRAKE.

gasket Canvas strip or other tying device to hold sail in place when furled and not in use; a stop; a tyer.

gather way See WAY.

gear 1. RIGGING on a boat. 2. Collection of items on a boat such as sails, ropes, anchor, pump, belongings, etc.

Different kinds of gear are specified as such. *Foul weather gear* is waterproof clothing for rain and heavy weather, usually consisting of a jacket and trousers. *Sailing gear* denotes all the articles that go with the sails—BATTENS, STOPS, REEFING ropes, sail bag, and so on.

Extra gear can include a limitless number of sailboat accessories. The minimum for safety includes:

anchor
extra rope (LINE) and some twine
knife
bailer (can or pump)
paddle (or oar)
life jackets or safety cushions for each person on board

Other items which a boat owner may want to carry— depending on the type of outing, how long he will be gone, how far he intends to sail, what the weather predictions are, etc.:

binoculars
boat hook
bucket
chart

cockpit cover
compass
extra   fittings—shackles,
        snap hooks, slides, etc.

GOOSENECK

fenders	pliers
first aid kit	radio
flares	sail bag
flashlight	screw driver
foghorn	sewing kit
food	sponge
foul weather gear	warm clothes
gloves for holding sheets	water jug
mending tape	whistle
outboard motor	

genoa, genoa jib Large jib, often nicknamed a "Jenny" or a "Ginny," usually for racing, and resembling a SPINNAKER since it overlaps the MAINSAIL and is controlled by ropes (SHEETS) outside all the RIGGING.

It is one of the LIGHT SAILS and is used to increase speed, primarily when CLOSE-HAULED and BEATING to WINDWARD. It is fastened to the JIBSTAY all along the leading edge (the LUFF), and also has a LEECH, whereas a spinnaker is held only at its three corners. See RIG and Fig. 35.

go about To change the boat's direction by turning into the wind; to come about; to tack. See COME ABOUT.

gooseneck Metal device which attaches the BOOM to the mast, allowing the boom to swing from side to side and usually also to slide up and down. See Fig. 13.

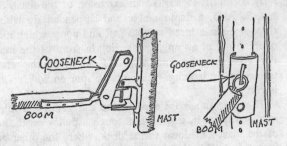

Figure 13. Goosenecks

77

goosewing jibe Accidental jibe in which only the bottom part of the sail goes over to the other side. See JIBE.

granny, granny knot Incorrectly made square knot. See KNOT.

grapnel Small anchor with several pointed arms (FLUKES) to use as a GRAPPLING IRON.

grappling iron Anchor to drag along the bottom of the ocean to recover lost articles, such as a MOORING or its parts.

grommet Metal ring or eyelet sewed on a sail to pass a rope through.

groove Slot running the length of the mast into which the rope-reinforced edge (LUFF) of the MAINSAIL is inserted and thus hoisted; often used instead of a SAIL TRACK. See MAST.

ground tackle All the necessary components of a mooring for securing a boat—anchor, chain, cable, etc. See MOORING.

gudgeon Eyebolt or socket attached to the stern of a boat (or on the RUDDER) into which the pins (PINTLES) on the rudder (or on the stern) fit, so that the rudder is demountable. See RUDDER.

gunter, sliding gunter 1. Small boat rig characterized by a four-sided sail laced to a top pole (GAFF) which is hung from the mast and pulled up almost perpendicularly so that it looks like an extension of the mast. See RIG. 2. Also, a demountable and suspended rig with a three-sided sail, laced to both gaff and BOOM which meet one another at an angle projecting in front of the mast; thus, the mast becomes a post from which the whole triangular rig is hung, rather than a spar on which a sail is run.

The HALYARD is fastened to the gaff about two-thirds of the way up it, then goes through a pulley on the top of the mast and down to the deck, where the other end is fastened. This rig is used widely on sailing canoes and

BOARD BOATS. It is essentially a LATEEN sail, though the latter has a longer gaff or YARD.

gunwale (pronounced "gunnel") Strengthening piece of wood all around the HULL where the deck meets the sides; rail.

gunwale guard Protective band around gunwale; rub rail.

guy Rope or wire that steadies a SPAR.

half hitch Single underhand loop around a taut piece of rope, a post, or other stationary object. See KNOT.

In fastening a rope (securing a LINE) to a CLEAT, a locking half hitch is often the final step: the top of the last figure eight (a loop) is turned over so that the end is "locked" under the loop as it is placed over the HORN of the cleat. The loop must then be lifted off the horn in order to release the line. See CLEAT.

halyard Rope (LINE) used to raise and lower a sail (in contrast to a SHEET, the rope used to pull in and let out a sail).

Each halyard is named according to the sail or part of the sail which it hoists: the *main halyard* is for the MAINSAIL; the *jib halyard* for the JIB. The halyard passes through a pulley (BLOCK) on the mast (for the mainsail at the top, for the jib at the JIBSTAY) with the two ends secured together when not in use.

Halyards are attached to sails by various devices. On small sailboats and DINGHIES the rope is often merely tied through the hole at the top (HEAD) of the sail; for handy attaching, a SNAP HOOK (Fig. 43) is often connected to the halyard; on larger, more expensive boats a SHACKLE is used.

When the sail has been raised, the other end of the halyard is secured to a CLEAT on the mast, COAMING, deck, or below deck. The halyards are sometimes run through blocks on the deck or mast, or through holes in the deck, before attaching. On a SLOOP the halyard on the left-hand (PORT) side of the mast is the jib halyard and the right-hand (STARBOARD) one, the main halyard. After cleating, coil the remaining rope and hang it by a loop on the cleat. See READYING, SAILBOAT PARTS.

hank   **1.** Small metal hooked fitting sewn into the edge of a sail to attach it to a STAY. See Plate 18. **2.** To attach or be attached to a stay, as the JIB *hanks* (or is *hanked*) to the JIBSTAY.

hard-alee   Words, or a command, used by a skipper to signify that he is pushing the TILLER over toward the sail (to the LEE side) to point the boat into the wind in order to come about (preceded by the command, "READY ABOUT!"). See COME ABOUT.

hard chine   See HULL.

harden   To remove the fluttering (LUFFING) up next to the mast in the sail by filling it with wind, either by heading the boat away from the wind or pulling in the sail.

hatch   Covered opening on a ship's deck for access to the inside of the boat.

haul   To pull, said of a rope; to change direction, said of the wind, usually in a counterclockwise direction. See VEER.

To *haul off* is to change one's course, to get away from something. To *haul the wind* is to turn the boat nearer the wind.

hawk   Wind indicator at the top of the mast; a fly.

hawser   Large rope.

head   **1.** Top corner of a three-sided (MARCONI RIG) sail. See SAILBOAT PARTS. **2.** Toilet on a yacht. **3.** To turn or steer your boat.

head away   Same as HEAD OFF.

headboard   Device at the top corner (HEAD) of a three-sided sail which strengthens it (usually by a piece of wood or metal inserted between the two layers of the cloth); it normally has a hole through which the HALYARD is inserted.

head down   To point the boat away from the direction of the wind (see Fig. 11); to head to LEEWARD; to go from a CLOSE-HAULED position to a REACHING or RUNNING position.

head into the wind To point the boat directly into the wind.

head off To point the boat farther away from the wind (usually from a CLOSE-HAULED position); to fall off; opposite of HEAD UP. See FALL OFF.

You head off when the sail is fluttering (LUFFING) in order to make it full, HARDEN it.

headsail Sail in front of the mast.

headstay Supporting wire running from the upper part of the mast to the bow. See FORESTAY.

head to wind With the bow facing the wind, said of a boat at a dock or MOORING. See Fig. 49.

When sails are being hoisted or lowered, your boat should always be head to wind.

head up To point the boat nearer the direction from which the wind is blowing; to point up; opposite of FALL OFF or HEAD OFF. See Fig. 11.

You head up into the wind to spill the wind out of the sail, if you are tipping (HEELING) too much.

headway Motion forward; opposite of STERNWAY.

As long as a boat has headway (or WAY on), the RUDDER can perform its function and the boat can be steered. A boat as it leaves the MOORING *gathers headway*.

heave to To point the bow into the wind and keep the boat as motionless as possible with the TILLER tied down, JIB backed and MAINSAIL pulled in; to stop, usually in case of emergency or too much wind.

heavy weather Strong winds with resultant rough water, white caps and squalls.

Heavy weather which consists of variable puffy winds may mean storms and danger ahead; a strong steady wind is less dangerous. Both can be taken in stride if you are prepared and your boat can take it. Heavy weather calls for: (1) The realization that you will get wet from spray and waves. (2) Foul weather GEAR, extra jackets, sweaters, etc. (3) A pump or bailing can for the water that comes in from the spray and even from HEELING. (4) Probably reducing your sail area by taking a REEF, or even lowering all sails if necessary. See REEF, STORM. (5) The application of some or all of the following hints on RIGGING and helmsmanship, which can help in heavy weather: (a) Flatten your MAINSAIL, so that it has very little POCKET or curve and will not catch and hold the wind but will LUFF sooner. Tighten it by pulling on the OUTHAUL and DOWNHAUL, and be sure the LEECH LINE is loose along the sail's outer edge so that it does not make a curve. (b) Keep your momentum (HEADWAY) and therefore your ability to control your boat. As long as you are able to make the boat react as needed, it can be handled to adjust to the puffs, the waves, and even the KNOCKDOWNS. See RUDDER. (c) When CLOSE-HAULED or BEATING, use the suggestions listed under HEELING—all weight to WINDWARD, spill the excessive wind out of the sail by pointing your boat up, or by letting out the MAINSHEET, or by both. A continual luff in your mainsail—sailing BY THE LUFF—keeps you moving with perhaps least strain; to accomplish this pull in the JIB tight but let the mainsail luff over most of its area. (d) When REACHING, the danger is that the boat may be rolled sideways by the waves, so be careful not to let the end of the BOOM dip into the water—you may lose control or be pulled over. Keep your crew to windward and farther back in the boat than for beating. (e) When RUNNING, be extra careful not to JIBE accidentally. This means you should make a series of BROAD REACHES or DOWNWIND TACKS rather than go directly before the wind. Be careful of getting turned sideways (BROACHING TO)—you can help to avoid this by dropping the CENTERBOARD and heading the boat a bit toward the wind when it rolls. Here too, keep your weight near the stern. (f) The waves kicked up by the wind can give you real trouble. By losing your wind and your headway when your boat is down in the trough of a wave, you are ready for a knockdown when you get up on the crest. Try to keep your boat moving by not bucking the waves directly and letting the boat ride as easily as possible. (g) COMING ABOUT and JIBING are both difficult and tricky. You may get caught IN IRONS coming about and you may hurt your sails or rigging in a jibe. So do both as little as possible, and don't jibe at all in a really big blow. Go from a run to a reach to a tack and then come about and return to your run again. See HEEL, JIBE.

heel 1. Lower end of a mast or SPAR. 2. Stern end of the KEEL. 3. Sideways tipping of a boat. 4. To tip, as a result of the wind against the sail.

The boat heels when the sail is pulled in and you are CLOSE-HAULED and BEATING. Most small boats sail better when they are heeling a bit toward the side the sail is on (to LEEWARD), but too much heel is not only frightening for a beginner; it also means you may take in water over the low side of the boat, that the danger of capsizing is increased, and that the boat is actually slowed down, as it is not designed to sail this way. And a boat with little or no momentum, without a flow of water past the RUDDER for it to act on, will not respond to the TILLER. See RUDDER.

To counteract excessive heeling you should: (1) Get all the weight possible (i.e., you and your crew) on the high (WINDWARD) side of the boat—sometimes HIKING STRAPS or TRAPEZES are used to get even farther out; on SCOWS, the crew rides the BILGE BOARDS. (2) Head into the wind to make the sail LUFF. (3) Let out the mainsheet thus "spilling the wind," which also makes the sail luff. See Fig. 14. (4) Be prepared in a really heavy wind to have a continual luff in the sail. (5) *Never cleat the mainsheet*.

Squally winds with sudden puffs mean that you and

① HIKE OUT TO WINDWARD

② HEAD INTO THE WIND
AND... OR...

③ SPILL WIND FROM SAIL

Figure 14. Heel

your crew must be alert. They must scramble up to the windward side when the boat begins to heel, but not stay there when the breeze suddenly drops (they may get wet seats).

A boat should seldom heel toward the side away from the sail (to windward). This means that in a light wind you must have some of your crew sitting on the DOWN side, as the force of the wind by itself is not strong enough to balance all the crew on the UP side. If you are sailing alone, you are the whole ballast and will probably have to break the rule that the skipper sits to windward and sit on the leeward side. See HEAVY WEATHER, HIKE.

helm Technically a boat's total steering apparatus including both TILLER and RUDDER, but in a small boat, more commonly the device grasped by the skipper to steer the boat—the tiller—and which then engages the underwater rudder. See RUDDER.

To *put the helm up* is to pull it toward the "high side," the side against which the wind is blowing, the WINDWARD side away from the sail. To *put the helm down* is to push it (since the helmsman is usually sitting to windward) toward the side of the boat the sail is on, the LEEWARD side.

A boat with a WEATHER HELM will tend to turn toward the direction the wind is coming from. If tiller and sails are let go, the boat will head into the wind by itself, an important safety factor. Your boat should have a slight weather helm, and the tiller a slight tendency to go to leeward.

A LEE HELM is the opposite and therefore a dangerous tendency—the boat wants to turn away from the wind and the helmsman must push the tiller to the LEE side continually to keep the boat on course. See WEATHER HELM.

helmsman Person at the TILLER (or wheel) who steers the boat; usually the skipper on a small boat.

helmsmanship Practice of the fine art of handling a boat.

high Toward the direction the wind is coming from, usually used with POINT or HEAD; to windward.

When BEATING you should try to *point as high as possible*, without letting your sails LUFF. You *head higher* on a beat than on a CLOSE REACH.

hike, hike out To climb or lean far out over the high side of the boat (to WINDWARD) to counteract excessive tipping (HEELING) while sailing to windward (BEATING). See BILGE BOARD, HEEL and Plate 22.

HIKING STRAPS and TRAPEZES are sometimes installed by racing skippers to aid in *hiking out,* or the crew stands on the bilge boards.

hiking stick Same as TILLER EXTENSION.

hiking strap Belt-like device firmly secured to the COCKPIT to enable the crew to HIKE OUT (usually by hooking their toes under the crosswise strap) when BEATING.

hitch Simple knot.

hoist To pull up, raise. See Plate 13.

horn 1. Prong of a cleat. 2. Arm of a jaw. 3. Holding device for an oar on a rowboat.

horse Same as TRAVELER.

housing That part of the mast below the deck.

hull Structural frame that forms the body of a boat as distinct from its sails, SPARS and RIGGING. See Fig. 40.

Although there are various types of hulls for small boats, the smaller the hull, the less important is its design. What might be best hydrodynamically can all too easily be nullified by too much or improperly distributed LIVE BALLAST.

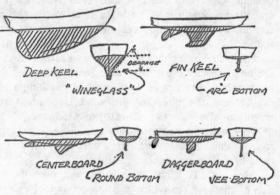

Figure 15. Hull Types and Keel

Most small boats have a "displacement" hull, but the "planing" hull is growing in popularity. The former plows through the water; the latter skims over it. Viewed horizontally, the bottom of a planing hull is flat with an upturned bow; cross-sectionally it is flat or has a slight arc. It has a "hard chine," that is, the sides and bottom meet at a sharp angle. A displacement hull has a V-shaped or round bottom, or a flat bottom that turns upward more at the stern and flares more at the sides than the planing hull. See CENTERBOARD, KEEL, SAILBOAT PARTS.

hurricane   See STORM SIGNALS.

I

inboard Inside the HULL; opposite of OUTBOARD.

in irons Headed directly into the wind, unable to go forward (make HEADWAY) or get started on either TACK; in stays.

Getting caught in irons can happen when COMING ABOUT, either because you were not going fast enough (FOOTING well) or because you did not push the TILLER far enough over to allow the wind to catch the other side of the sail, or you brought it back too soon once you had pushed it over. It may also happen in getting away from a MOORING, or in BEATING, especially in heavy weather.

Here are some suggestions on what to do if you are in irons: (1) Pull—even jerk—the tiller toward you briskly three or four times, but be sure to push it *slowly* back to the center between each pull. (2) Grasp the JIB by its back corner (the CLEW) and pull it to the opposite side from which you wish to turn (BACKWIND the jib); that is, pull it to STARBOARD if you want the bow to go to PORT, and vice versa. (3) If you are actually going backward (MAKING STERNWAY), put the tiller to the side toward which you wish to turn. (This is just the opposite of what you would normally do—pull the tiller to the side away from the direction you wish to go in—because when you are moving backward the action of the tiller and rudder is reversed.) See RUDDER. (4) If you have no jib, or if you are alone and cannot get to it, push the BOOM out to one side (backwind the main-

91

sail). See Fig. 16. (5) Of course, a few strokes of an oar or a paddle can also get you out of irons, and although it may not be regarded as very nautical, don't hesitate to do this if you are drifting toward any sort of obstacle.

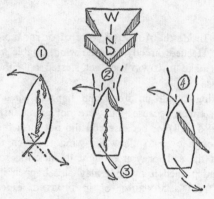

Figure 16. In Irons

in stays Same as IN IRONS.

insurance Prudent thing for the boat owner to have.

With the growing number of sailing enthusiasts, it is more important than ever that the small boat owner carry insurance. Consult your agent concerning the various different kinds and which is the best for you.

international code Code of flag signals used throughout the world to communicate between boats and from ship to shore.

The system consists of twenty-six letter flags (one for each letter of the alphabet), ten number flags (one, two, three, etc.), three repeater flags, and an answering pennant. Each letter flag is also assigned a name (i.e., the A flag is also called Alfa, B is Bravo, C is Charlie) as well as a special message: for instance, displayed alone the D flag means "Keep clear of me—I am maneuvering with difficulty," the C flag, "Yes," and the N flag, "No," the O flag, "Man overboard." The code includes signals in combination up to as many as four letter flags. (See booklet H. O. No. 87, of the Hydrographic Office, Navy Department, Washington, D.C.)

International Code flags are also flown all at once to decorate a ship on national holidays or at regattas and on special occasions, but only when the boat is at anchor. See FLAG.

Irish pennant Frayed rope end; loose rope; cow's-tail.
irons See IN IRONS.

J

jaw, jaws Semicircular or U-shaped end on a BOOM (or GAFF) by which it fits around the mast, slides up and down, and swings from side to side; it serves the same purpose as a GOOSENECK. See Fig. 12 under GAFF for illustration.

jib Triangular sail in front of the mast which, added to the MAINSAIL, differentiates the two-sailed SLOOP from the one-sailed CATBOAT.

The jib is hoisted up the JIBSTAY (see Plate 17) by the jib HALYARD, and once up is pulled in and out (TRIMMED) usually by two jib SHEETS attached to the CLEW of the sail, one on the STARBOARD side, one on the PORT. The WINDWARD one is left free and uncleated, the LEEWARD one (on the same side as the sails) is made fast to a CLEAT on the deck. (On some boats a TRAVELER in front of the mast allows one jib sheet to do the job.)

Just how far in the jib should be trimmed must be learned by experience. If too far in, it will push the wind against the back side of the mainsail and cause it to LUFF. If too far out, the jib itself will luff and lose part of its effectiveness. To find the right trim, pull it in to a point at which the mainsail just shivers (from the BACKWIND of the jib) and then let it out just enough to allow the mainsail to be full—this should be the right place to cleat it. See BEAT, JIB HALYARD, JIB SHEET, READYING, RIG, SAILBOAT PARTS.

jibe 1. Act of jibing. 2. In RUNNING or sailing before the wind, to turn the boat's stern so that the wind comes on the other side of the sail, thus crossing behind rather than in front of the boat; the opposite of COMING ABOUT or TACKING. See Fig. 17.

A jibe can be either planned or unplanned. There is nothing dangerous about a well-executed, planned jibe— a necessary and pleasurable performance almost every time you go sailing—but a jibe that takes you by surprise, especially in a strong wind, can be disastrous. This happens when the skipper fails to realize that the wind has crossed his stern and is now blowing on the *same* side as the sail is on.

A planned jibe takes place because you want to change your direction and go more to LEEWARD (or perhaps the wind has changed), and so you must get the sail on the other side of the boat. You *could* do this by turning all the way into the wind and coming about, but because you are headed so far away from the wind, this would be almost a complete circle, a waste of time and motion (unless you feel that a jibe will be dangerous). Therefore you will turn your stern just a bit so that the wind crosses it; then, since wind and sail cannot both be on the same side of the boat, the sail must also cross. Because sail, SHEET and BOOM are way out on one side, they have a long way to go, and they go there in a hurry. In tacking, by contrast, the sail only has half as far to go, and that edge of the sail past which the wind passes (the LUFF) is fastened all along its length to the mast, and so flutters gradually over. In jibing, the wind catches the LEECH, which is attached to nothing, and whips it over with a hard jerk and without the loss of momentum of the tack. So for a planned jibe, use these steps: (1) Prepare your crew with the words, "Ready to jibe" (or "Stand by to jibe") and then as you start to carry out the jibe, call out, "Jibe-ho" (or "Jibing over"). (2) As you do this, head your bow slowly away from the wind (pull the TILLER toward you, away from the sail). (3) At the same time, haul (or have your crew haul) in on the MAINSHEET rapidly hand over hand, so that the sail

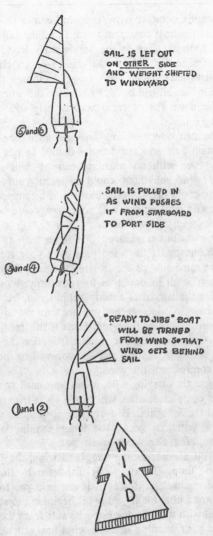

SAIL IS LET OUT
ON OTHER SIDE
AND WEIGHT SHIFTED
TO WINDWARD

⑤and⑥

SAIL IS PULLED IN
AS WIND PUSHES
IT FROM STARBOARD
TO PORT SIDE

③and④

"READY TO JIBE" BOAT
WILL BE TURNED
FROM WIND SO THAT
WIND GETS BEHIND
SAIL

①and②

W
I
N
D

Figure 17. Jibing

is over the COCKPIT when the wind comes DEAD ASTERN. (4) As the boat continues to turn and the sail goes over, shift your BALLAST to the windward side. (5) Let out the mainsheet quickly on the other side. (6) If you have RUNNING BACKSTAYS, don't forget to loosen the one on the side the sail will be on and tighten the other. (7) You can let down the CENTERBOARD to help steady the boat during a jibe.

You can now see how an unplanned jibe, in which the mainsheet and sail are *not* hauled in but crash violently over with no warning, can be dangerous. In a heavy wind, anything could happen: your sheet and rigging could break, your mast could be snapped in two, you could capsize, you and your crew could be knocked on the head, or overboard.

To avoid an unplanned jibe never sail BY THE LEE, that is, never let the wind pass over your stern and be on the same side of the boat as the sail. The answer, if you are at all in doubt, is to TACK DOWNWIND, that is, to have the wind not exactly behind you, but a little to the windward side, so that you are sure the sail is on the opposite side from the wind. Even if this means you are not heading exactly for your destination and have to make a couple of jibed zigzags, you will be the one who is in control, not the wind.

If you are carrying a jib, it can wait until your planned jibe is completed, after which the jib is trimmed on the leeward side again. However, if it is held WUNG-OUT with a WHISKER POLE, the latter should be removed before jibing. See WING AND WING.

If you are not sailing wing and wing, the jib will be hanging limply because it is blanketed by the mainsail and seems useless. However, it can help you to avoid an unplanned jibe, for if you see it beginning to shift across and fill with wind on the opposite side from the mainsail, that is your warning that the wind has gotten around in back of the mainsail and may soon cause it to cross over to the other side. Head the boat toward the wind (by pushing the tiller down to leeward, away from you) to bring the wind back on the right side of the sail.

A *flying jibe* occurs when the mainsail is not pulled in and the sail slams over from way out on one side to way out on the other side.

A *goosewing jibe* occurs when the boom goes across but the top part of the sail does not, and your mainsail is divided by the mast into two "goose wings." The best way out of this predicament is to jibe back and start over, as it is almost impossible to force either half of the sail over to the other side. See BY THE LEE, RUN, TACK DOWNWIND.

jibe-ho Command used by the skipper to signify that he is starting the act of JIBING (preceded by the command, "Ready to jibe"). See JIBE.

jib halyard Rope (LINE) by which the JIB is pulled up and down.

It is attached to the top (HEAD) of the jib with a knot or a SNAP HOOK. The front edge (LUFF) of the jib is fastened to the wire JIBSTAY and hauled up along this by the halyard. The other (or pulling) end of the halyard is then fastened on a CLEAT at the left side of the mast and coiled neatly. When you lower and remove (UNBEND) the jib, be sure *both* ends of the halyard are well secured (every sailor has his own favorite method). See HALYARD, READYING, SAILBOAT PARTS.

jib-headed rig, jib-headed sail Rig with a triangular sail, so named because it is shaped like a JIB, in contrast to the four-sided GAFF type; a Marconi rig; a Bermuda rig.

jib sheet Rope (there is usually one on each side) by which the JIB is pulled in and let out (TRIMMED) after it has been hoisted.

The two jib sheets—one for the STARBOARD side, one for the PORT—are attached together to the lower back corner (the CLEW) of the jib, by a knot or a SNAP HOOK. The jib is controlled with the LEEWARD jib sheet, the one on the same side as the MAINSAIL. Be sure the other one (the WINDWARD sheet) does not get caught or tangled as you change the sail from one side to the other (COME ABOUT). The only exception to the rule of managing the jib with the leeward sheet is when you are RUNNING dead before the wind in a WING AND WING position with the jib on the opposite side from the mainsail; then you will use the windward jib sheet to keep the jib WUNG-OUT.

The jib sheets are led backward through FAIRLEADS or BLOCKS on the deck to their CLEATS. This is a handy place for a *jam* or a *cam* cleat with their speedy rope release mechanisms. A figure eight KNOT in the end of the sheet will keep it from slipping out of the fairlead, should you happen to let go of it. See READYING, SAILBOAT PARTS.

jibstay Wire running from the upper part of the mast to the bow, to which the JIB is attached; forestay; headstay. See FORESTAY.

Because this STAY is the front support of the mast, it plays an important part in the trim of the boat and should be tight. See TRIM, WEATHER HELM. A loose jibstay may also prevent the jib from performing correctly, if the stay is sagging backward.

jigger Mast at the back of a boat, especially the small rear mast on a YAWL or KETCH; the mizzenmast; also the sail set on this mast.

jumper stay Short STAY running from the top of the mast to a STRUT.

jury Anything temporary, to be used as a makeshift, usually in an emergency; as a *jury rig* or *jury rudder*.

K

kedge 1. Small anchor. 2. To pull forward a boat (that has gone aground or is in a narrow channel) by tossing out an anchor and pulling the boat up to it. See ANCHOR.

keel 1. "Backbone" of the boat, the bottommost timber extending along its whole length and from which the HULL is built up. 2. Fixed and weighted fin or blade projecting well below the boat which prevents its sliding sideways (making LEEWAY) from wind pressure and lowers its center of gravity.

Small sailboats typically do not have a keel (they carry a CENTERBOARD or DAGGERBOARD), but there are keel class boats from 12 feet up. See ONE-DESIGN CLASS BOAT.

A keel gives a boat great stability and lateral resistance and does not have to be raised or lowered with changes in direction of the boat. However, because it *is* fixed, it always needs at least two feet of water, so that the owner of a keel boat will have less flexibility than a centerboard-boat sailor in MOORING, transporting, winter storage, and exploring unknown waters. If enough water should come in over the sides in HEAVY WEATHER, a keel boat can swamp and even sink. Therefore, extra flotation devices are necessary. See CHOOSING A BOAT.

There are two main types of keel: a *fin keel* and a *deep keel*. Most small and medium-sized class boats have the fin keel, which is a weighted "fin" shaped much like a centerboard and projecting only below the middle part of the hull. See HULL. The deep keel lies along the hull's bottom, tapering down at its deepest point so that

101

a cross-section view looks like a wineglass. See Fig. 15.

keelson Lengthwise timber over the keel inside the boat.

ketch Two-masted boat, the smaller mast (the MIZZEN-MAST) being behind (AFT of) the taller mainmast but in front (FORWARD) of the TILLER. See RIG.

kick-up rudder Rudder on a small boat which is attached to the back of the TRANSOM, and the lower half of which will pivot up for shallow water, low tide and beaching. See RUDDER.

kit boat Parts of a boat, packaged and ready for the sailor to assemble and finish in the long winter months.

kite Nickname for a PARACHUTE SPINNAKER.

knockabout 1. Small sailboat. 2. Cape Cod knockabout, a type of class boat. See ONE-DESIGN CLASS BOAT.

knockdown Extreme tipping (HEELING) due to a sudden puff of wind or squall; the "blow" that causes the boat to capsize.

Only a KEEL boat will recover from a knockdown without capsizing. Avoid a knockdown by watching the wind, by keeping your boat moving forward, and by LUFFING. See HEAVY WEATHER, HEEL.

knot 1. Nautical unit of speed—6080 feet or one nautical mile per hour.

Since a nautical mile is longer than a land mile (5280 feet), *making ten knots* is faster than ten mph. Because a knot is a unit of *speed,* not distance, it is incorrect to say "ten knots per hour"—the per hour is understood. 2. Tie or fastening in a rope; a bend; a hitch.

There are over 15,000 knots you could learn while becalmed, but only a few are needed by the small boat sailor. Knowledge of knots is important for several reasons—for security, for convenience, for appearance. Tying knots is really quite easy—after all, most people have learned to tie their shoelaces. Begin by taking a piece of small rope or LINE and learn the following few terms. A rope has three sections: (1) The *end* (working end, or fall) of the rope is the section you work with in tying a knot. (2) The *standing part* is the inactive section of the rope. (3) The *bight* is the curving section between the end and the standing part. See Fig. 18. When two sections of a rope cross each other, one must go over and the other under. It is an *overhand loop* when the end crosses over the standing part, and an *underhand loop* when the end crosses under the standing part. See Fig. 18.

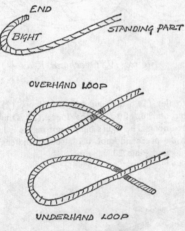

Figure 18. Knot

The term *drawing up* refers to the tightening up of the sections of the rope once the knot has been formed. Unless the knot is drawn up evenly and carefully, a miserable tangle may result.

Knowledge of knots, like all knowledge, is useless without application. Therefore when studying knots one should learn their names, when to use them, and how to tie them. The six basic knots explained here are: *overhand, figure eight, square, bowline, clove hitch, slipped ring.*

103

Overhand knot. The overhand knot is usually tied near the end of a rope to prevent it from fraying, or slipping through a hole. It is simple and fast to tie, and it is compact. It should be used when you are not concerned about untying—it is hard to untie. See Fig. 19.

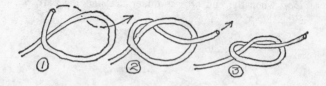

Figure 19. Overhand Knot

How to tie: (1) Make an overhand loop. (2) Circle the end under and up through the loop. (3) Draw up tight.

Figure eight knot. The figure eight knot makes a larger "stopper" than the overhand knot. It is stronger and easier to untie. See Fig. 20 and Plate 20.

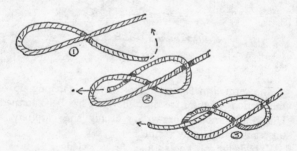

Figure 20. Figure Eight Knot

How to tie: (1) Make an underhand loop. (2) Circle the end around the standing part and up through the loop. (3) Draw up tight.

Square knot. The square or reef knot is widely used to tie together two lines of the same size or the two ends of the same line, which has been wrapped around a bundle of some sort, such as a furled sail. It is a treacherous knot, however, since it may loosen if the two ropes being tied together are not the same size, or if it is not properly tied. It then becomes what is popularly known as a granny knot. See Fig. 21.

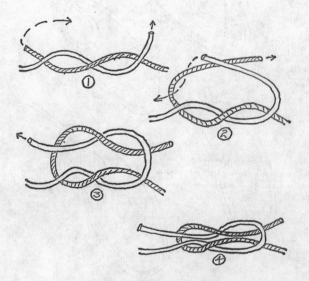

Figure 21. Square or Reef Knot

How to tie: (1) Take the two ends, one in each hand. Pass the left end over and around under the right end and point it up. (2) Cross what is now the left end under the right end. (3) Pass what is now the right end over and around the left end through the loop. (4) Draw up tight.

Bowline. The bowline is used to tie a line to a ring, an anchor, or a mast, or whenever a strong non-slip loop is desired. It does not jam or slide and is easy to untie. See Fig. 22.

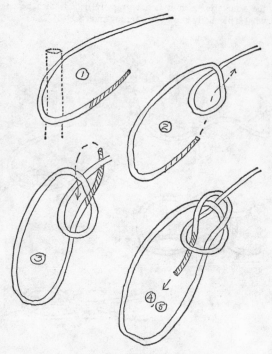

Figure 22. Bowline

How to tie: (1) Pass the end around the object to be tied. (2) Make an overhand loop on the standing part. (3) Pass the end up through the loop and behind the standing part. (4) Curve the end around under the standing part and pass it down through the loop. (5) Holding the standing part in one hand and the end in the other, draw up tight.

[1] *Under way*

[2] *Do NOT step into a boat this way*

[3] *Because this is what happens*

[4] *Step into the middle of the boat*

[5] *And keep a firm hold on the gunwale
and your weight low*

[6] *Stepping the mast*

[7] *Securing the shrouds*

[8] *Attaching the rudder*

[9] *Lowering the daggerboard*

[10] *Figure eight knot holds the halyard in the head of the sail*

[11] *Sail slides on sail track—ready to hoist*

[12] *Sheet is passed through boom block*

[13] *Hoisting the sail*

[14] *Coiling the halyard*

[15] *Pulling a loop through the coil*

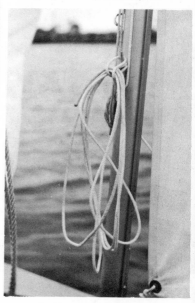

[16] *Coil hung by loop on mast cleat*

[17] *Jib is attached to jibstay—*

[18] *By hanks*

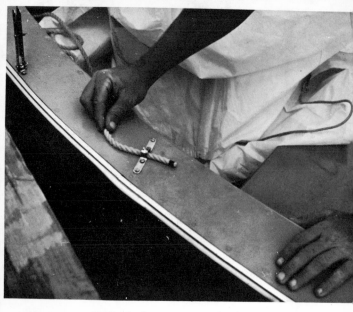

[19] *Jib sheet is run through fairlead*

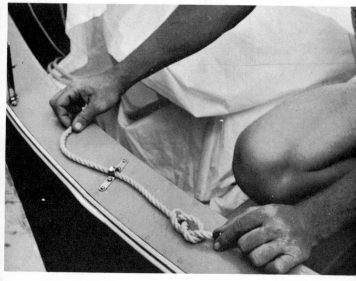

[20] *Figure eight knot is used as a stopper*

[21] *Beating to windward on the port tack*

[22] *Hiking out on the starboard tack*

[23] *Off on a port reach*

[24] *Close reach showing slot effect*

[25] *Running*

[26] *Wing and wing*

[27] *Spinning along with a spinnaker*

[28] *Spinnaker pole on opposite side from boom*

[29] *On the leeward leg*

[30] *Use of jib sheet well trimmed (left);*
stopper knot forgotten (right)

[31] *Who has the right of way?*

[32] *Both on the port tack—which is the privileged boat?*

[33] *Sail luffing when coming about*

[34] *Crew shifting to windward after coming about*

[35] *Capsized*

[36] *Turned turtle*

[37] *Righting*

[38] *Standing on daggerboard*

[39] *Dropping the mainsail*

[40] *Stability (due to buoyant foam in sides)*

[41] *Steer with the tiller while being towed ashore*

[42] *Dumping is easier than bailing*

[43] *On the beach*

[44] *Pushing off*

[45] *Four boats being towed*

[46] *Becalmed*

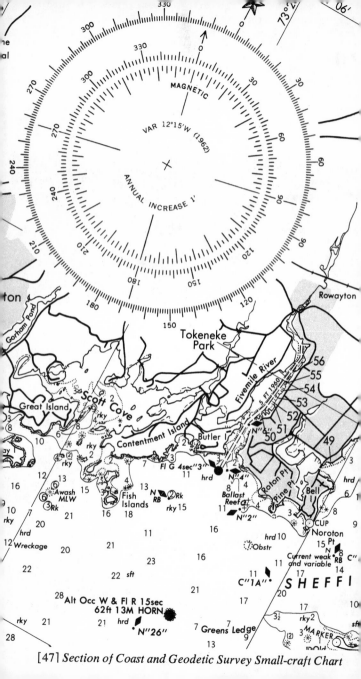

[47] *Section of Coast and Geodetic Survey Small-craft Chart*

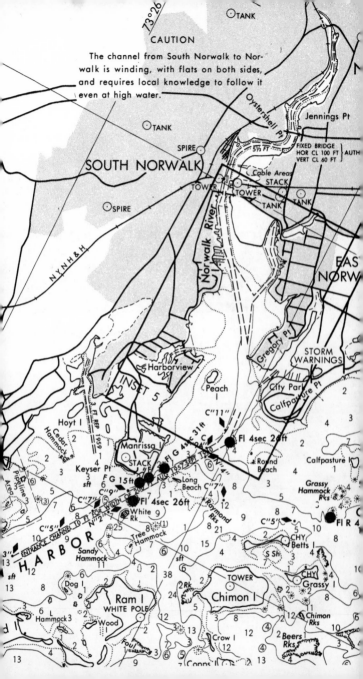

73°26

⊙TANK

CAUTION

The channel from South Norwalk to Norwalk is winding, with flats on both sides,
and requires local knowledge to follow it
even at high water.

⊙TANK

Oystershell Pt

Jennings Pt

5½ FT

FIXED BRIDGE
HOR CL 100 FT
VERT CL 60 FT
AUTH

SPIRE ⊙

Cable Areas
STACK

SOUTH NORWALK

TOWER ⊙
TOWER ⊙

⊙SPIRE

TANK TANK

N Y N H & H

Norwalk River

EAS
NORW

Gregory Pt

STORM
WARNINGS

Harborview

INSET 5

Peach

City Park
Calfpasture Pt

C"11"

Hoyt I

3 FT REP 1959

Fl 4sec 26ft

Calfpasture

Manrissa I

STACK
F2 F G 4sec 31ft

Round
Beach

Keyser Pt

F G 15ft

Grassy
Hammock
Rks

Long
Beach C"11"

Pipeline

Area

C"7" C"9"

Fl 4sec 26ft

Raymond
Rks

White
Rk

C"5"

FI R 4

C"5"

N"2"

Tree
Hammock

CHY
Betts I

HARBOR

Sandy
Hammock

S Sh

3"

sft

Dog I

TOWER

CHY
Grassy

Ram I
WHITE POLE

Chimon I

Chimon
Rks

Hammock

Wood

Crow I

Beers
Rks

[48] *Heading into the wind to make a landing*

[49] *Jib is lowered first*

[50] *Boats in use for outboarding, sailing, and rowing*

[51] *Speedsters*

[52] *Rowing—beginning the pull*

[53] *Rowing—too much arm pull in relation to back posture!*

[54] *Rowing—ready for a turn*

[55] *Rowing—turning around*

[56] *Ready to pump*

[57] *Always leave your boat dry*

[58] *Sculling—wrist down*

[59] *Sculling—wrist straight*

[60] *Sculling—wrist over*

[61] *Up from the dock*

[62] *Placing boat on trailer*

Clove hitch. The clove hitch (sometimes referred to as "a couple of half hitches") is a quick way to tie a line to a post (there must be tension on the standing part to make it hold fast). See Fig. 23.

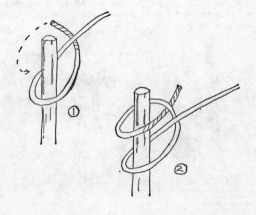

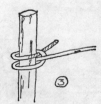

Figure 23. Clove Hitch

How to tie: (1) Make an underhand loop around the post. (2) Drop another underhand loop over the post. (3) Draw up tight.

107

Slipped ring knot. (Also called a "slipped half hitch," "a halter hitch," or simply "a noose.") This knot has several uses. It is excellent for tying a rope (such as a PAINTER) to a ring; for tying up to a post, since it holds tight without requiring the tension needed for a clove hitch; and for use in place of a bowline. The fact that it can be slipped along the standing part of the rope to make it fit snugly next to whatever it is being tied to (for example, a HALYARD to the HEAD of a sail) means that it sometimes is preferable to the non-slip bowline. See Fig. 24.

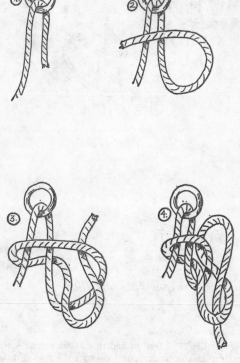

Figure 24. Slipped Ring Knot

How to tie: (1) Put the rope through the ring, holding the end parallel to the standing part. (2) Make an overhand loop where the two ropes lie side by side. (3) Pass the end over the standing part, down and under; then with your thumb and forefinger reach down through the loop and pull another loop up through it. (4) Draw up tight by pulling on the last loop. Now, if you pull on the end, the knot unties immediately. In order to prevent the knot from untying by itself, put the end through the last loop or bight. Then when you come to untie it, just take the end out of the bight and pull briskly.

L

labor To roll and pitch heavily in a rough sea, said of a boat.

lacing Rope used to tie a sail to a pole (SPAR) such as the BOOM or GAFF. See Fig. 12.

land To bring a boat up to a dock, MOORING, or other stopping place, accessible to the land. See LANDING.

land breeze Breeze that blows from the land to the sea.

landing Place to bring a boat up to, accessible to land.

Making a landing is the act of maneuvering your boat up to such a place.

Making a landing is more difficult than getting under way (see UNDER WAY) because of the extra factors of timing and precision involved. Whether you are arriving at a dock, a float, or a MOORING, your objective is the same: to have the boat stop at just the moment you come to your landing place. You must, as always, be alert to the direction and strength of the wind.

Because the wind blowing against the sail is what makes your boat go, by the same token, if the sail is immobilized because the wind is not pushing against it, but blowing on both sides of it at once, the boat will not be going forward. This happens when the boat is pointing bow first into the wind (HEAD TO WIND) with the BOOM in the middle of the boat (AMIDSHIPS); and this is how you want to end up when you make a landing. See Plate 48.

You cannot sail "full tilt" directly to your landing place, even though it is straight ahead of you. You must come up to it from "behind"—from DOWNWIND or LEE-

WARD—and allow time and space before you reach it to turn the boat from its sailing position—whether a RUN, a REACH or a BEAT—around up into the wind. Even then it will not stop immediately, but coast along on its momentum (SHOOT). The amount of shoot varies with the boat, its speed, and the wind, and is something you must learn by practice and experience with your own boat. Test it by throwing a stick or other object into the water as a substitute mooring.

Landing at a mooring ("fetching a mooring"). Although each boat has its own shoot, the rule of thumb is that small CENTERBOARD boats will shoot about two or three boat lengths in a medium wind. Let us say you are sitting on the side of your boat opposite the sail (to WINDWARD), heading for your mooring on a reach—the easiest course from which to make a landing:

(1) As you approach, pull the TILLER toward you to head the boat away from the wind (FALL OFF) so that you are to leeward of the mooring buoy by two or three boat lengths.

(2) When the wind and you and the mooring are all directly in line with one another, push the tiller away from you fairly briskly to turn the boat straight toward the wind, letting go of the SHEETS at the same time.

(3) As the sail and boom come over the center of the boat, bring the tiller back amidships so that you do not keep on going around, but keep the boat facing head to wind.

(4) The shoot will (hopefully) take you to your mooring buoy where your crew, ready in the bow, will pick it up. See Fig. 25.

If you have underestimated your speed and distance and come rushing at the buoy, don't wrench an arm out trying to hold onto it, but let go, sail away a little distance, and try again; if the opposite occurs—your shoot is insufficient and you don't reach the buoy at all—you will, of course, have no choice but to try again. And one

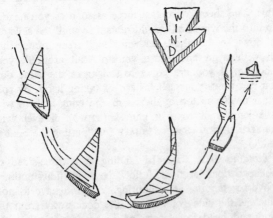

..... MAKING A LANDING, ALWAYS TURN
INTO THE WIND AND "SHOOT" FOR
YOUR OBJECTIVE; COASTING WITH
SAILS LUFFING.

Figure 25. Landing at a Mooring

last word: don't forget to make allowance for any current at your mooring (or dock).

To fetch a mooring when you are beating and the sail is in tight (CLOSE-HAULED), go a bit farther than you normally would on the last TACK before you come about to head for the mooring buoy so that you can come up to it on a reach as outlined above.

If you are sailing with the wind directly behind you (running), you must sail past the buoy in order to turn all the way around in a half-circle and come back up to it with your bow pointing directly into the wind. Keep the sail on the side away from the mooring so that you do not have to worry about JIBING.

While your crew is tying the boat to the mooring and taking the DINGHY back to tie it to the stern of the sailboat, get the sails down (JIB first) as quickly as possible. The sheets were cast loose as soon as you headed up into the wind and should remain so until the sails are all down so that the latter will "flap" freely rather than fill with wind and cause you to "sail around" your mooring. If you are going to sail again the same day, you can FURL your sail instead of taking it off, by rolling it neatly on top of the boom and tying it there with little lengths of rope or canvas (STOPS) or even with the MAINSHEET. (See SHIPSHAPE for "putting the boat to bed.")

Landing at a dock. In landing at a three-sided or T-shaped dock or float, follow the suggestions outlined above for landing at a mooring. You will have to note which is the side (or end) of the dock away from the wind and head to leeward of it. As you calculate the proper distance before turning into the wind to shoot toward the dock, remember that it is better to undershoot here, since a dock is an "immovable object" and you do not want to ram it. You can usually head for the side so as not to take it head on. Have your crew sitting down at the bow ready to fend off, with legs rather than arms. When the wind is blowing against the dock and obstacles are such that you have no space in which to make a HEAD-TO-WIND landing, you can come to within a few feet of the dock, let your sheets loose so the sail LUFFS, head into the wind to stop, and then drift to the dock, getting your sails down as soon as possible. Or, anchor several feet away, let your sails down, and paddle in (come in under BARE POLES). See Fig. 26.

landlubber What a sailor calls a non-sailor.

lanyard 1. Cord around a sailor's neck, usually for his knife (or stop watch, if racing). 2. Small piece of rope used to tie anything on a boat. 3. Rope strung through a deadeye (a round piece of wood with holes in it for ropes) used to lengthen or extend a wire support (STAY).

lapstreak Type of HULL construction in which the boards overlap; clinker-built; opposite of CARVEL-BUILT.

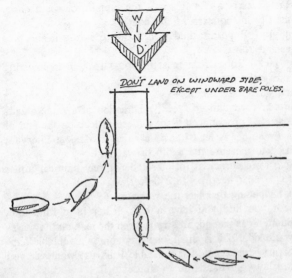

Figure 26. Landing at a Dock

larboard Obsolete term for the left (PORT) side of a ship.

lash To secure by binding with a rope, as to *lash the tiller*.

lateen, lateener Sailing rig originating in the Mediterranean Sea, made up of a three-sided sail on a long pole (YARD) slung from a low mast; essentially a sliding GUNTER rig. See RIG.

launch 1. Type of powerboat. 2. To set afloat.

lay 1. To twist the strands of a rope together to make a rope. 2. Direction in which the strands of a rope are twisted around each other. 3. To succeed in attaining your goal without TACKING. 4. To go or come, as to *lay aloft,* to *lay forward.*

To *lay to* is to turn a boat into the wind and keep it there; to stop a boat; to lie to. *To lay up* is to take out of the water, as of a boat for the winter.

115

lazaret, lazarette Small space for supplies or spare parts, usually in the stern of the boat.

lazy guy Rope attached to a BOOM to steady it and prevent a JIBE.

lazy jack Rope from mast to BOOM to help in lowering and gathering in sail.

leach Same as LEECH.

lead 1. (pronounced "leed") Direction of a rope; a fairlead. 2. (pronounced "led") Piece of lead on the end of a *lead line*. A lead line is a rope, marked at intervals, used to measure the depth of water.

league Measurement of distance, three nautical miles (3 × 6080 feet, or 18,240 feet).

leak Opening that lets the water in.

If you find you have a leak, better head for shore, pumping as you go, and try to keep the leak on the WINDWARD side. If it is small, chewing gum is a valuable temporary stopper. If it is a sizable leak, use whatever you can lay your hands on to stuff into it.

lee 1. Away from the direction from which the wind is blowing; to leeward; opposite of WEATHER or WINDWARD. See DIRECTION. (If the wind is blowing against the STARBOARD side of the boat, the PORT side is the lee side.) 2. Protected spot; if you are *in the lee* of some object, you are protected by it from the wind.

leeboard Board attached, one on each side of a boat, which serves instead of a CENTERBOARD, the LEEWARD being lowered to retard the sideways slipping (LEEWAY) of the boat when CLOSE-HAULED.

The leeboards are carried on the outside of the HULL, usually attached by bolts on which they pivot. The lower end may also be raised and lowered by a TACKLE. They are used especially on sailing canoes where they are attached to a special THWART, AMIDSHIPS. See BILGE BOARD.

leech Outside edge of a sail farthest from the mast. See SAILBOAT PARTS.

116

leech line Rope sewed into the LEECH of a sail to regulate its amount of curve or POCKET.

It can usually be left alone, but if the sail is too flat or curves backward or if you are in a light wind, it may be tightened to make more of a bag in the sail to catch the wind. Be sure it is *not* pulled up to pucker the sail in a heavy wind when a flat sail is needed.

lee helm Dangerous tendency of a boat to turn away from the direction the wind is coming from. See WEATHER HELM.

lee shore Shore facing the LEE side of a boat; shore onto which a wind is blowing.

leeward (pronounced "loord") Away from the direction of the wind; on the LEE side; down; opposite of WINDWARD and WEATHER.

The sail and BOOM are always on the leeward side of the boat. See DIRECTION and Plate 29.

leeway Sideways movement of a boat away from the wind (to LEEWARD), as a result of the pressure of the wind, when it is not counterbalanced by the CENTERBOARD or KEEL sufficiently to keep the boat from slipping sideways somewhat.

A boat *makes leeway* when it sideslips. If you try to sail your boat CLOSE-HAULED without lowering the centerboard, you will make leeway almost as fast as you make HEADWAY. Even with the centerboard down there is some normal leeway.

leg 1. Distance traveled on one TACK before COMING ABOUT. 2. That part of a course or a race between two markers. See COURSE.

leg-of-mutton Three-sided sail.

light air Soft breeze, sometimes becoming none at all; sailor's name for light wind.

Lack of wind can be even worse than too much wind. Here are a few things to try in light air:

(1) If you are sailing into the wind (BEATING), be extra careful not to pull in the sails too tight (to PINCH);

117

in fact, try sailing a bit farther away from (OFF) the wind than usual. And be sure your human ballast (you and your crew) is placed so that the boat tips (HEELS) a bit toward the side of the boat the sail is on (to LEE-WARD). Lengthwise, the weight should be as near the middle as possible.

(2) Make the sail have as much curve or POCKET as possible to catch the wind—by loosening the corners (OUTHAUL and DOWNHAUL) a bit and tightening the LEECH LINE (if you have one) along the back edge of the sail to put a curve in it. You can even take out one or more BATTENS.

(3) On a REACH or a RUN, try unfastening the MAIN-SHEET from the TRAVELER so that letting out and pulling in the sail is accomplished with only one length of rope and a minimum of friction. Keep the BOOM held out with an arm or a pole.

(4) Have your crew practice "slow motion," or better still, don't let them move around in the boat at all. Quick jerky movement (or even any motion) will spill whatever wind there is out of the sail.

(5) Stay low in the boat so that every little bit of wind can reach the sail unimpeded.

(6) Watch to see where the little breezes—CATSPAWS—are coming from. Don't go too close to the shore and be caught in the LEE of the land. And remember the wind tends to die down at sunset.

(7) If you are caught in a dead calm, you will be glad you followed the rule always to carry an oar or a paddle. A floorboard or even a pair of hands can be used in a pinch; pushing the TILLER back and forth also helps.

(8) As darkness falls, don't be too proud to take a tow from an outboard motor.

lights Same as on land.

If you are going to be doing any night sailing, you should know: (1) the rules and regulations concerning lights on boats, and (2) the lights used in our navigational system.

Boat lights. A green light on the right (STARBOARD) and a red light on the left (PORT) made to show from dead AHEAD to two POINTS (see COMPASS) ABAFT THE BEAM, must be carried by sailboats at night. (Sailboats under 18 feet may use a flashlight or preferably a lantern having a red glass on one side and a green on the other.) So if you see both a green and a red light coming toward you, it means a boat is approaching you head on, while if only a green light is visible, you are looking at the starboard side of a boat. Small sailboats should carry a flashlight anyway to shine on the sail—for overtaking, to avoid collision, and in case they lack the red and green lantern. Power-driven boats carry white lights, called range lights, in the front and back, in addition to port and starboard lights.

Navigation lights. As you enter a harbor, the lights marking the right-hand side of the channel are red, and the ones on the left are green. ("Red, right returning" comes into use here. See BUOY.) Sometimes white is used in combination with the colors, as it shows up better. Lighthouses and certain buoys have special types of flashing and occulting lights, each with its own pattern, which are marked on the CHARTS for identification by sailors. A fixed light is continuous, a flashing light has longer periods of darkness than light, and an occulting light has longer periods of light than darkness.

light sails Sails lighter in weight and usually for lighter winds than the WORKING SAILS; the SPINNAKER, the GENOA JIB and the REACHING JIB are the light sails, usually used for increasing speed and therefore primarily for racing.

Though the regular MAINSAIL and JIB are usually made of Dacron nowadays, nylon has remained the favorite material for the light sails, because it *is* light and yet tightly woven too.

lightship Stationary vessel with special markings and a powerful light of known characteristics used as an aid to navigation.

limber holes Holes in cross boards (RIBS) near the bottom of the boat to allow water to flow from one place to another and be pumped or bailed out.

line Sailor's preferred word for almost all ropes on a boat. The most important lines are called SHEETS and HALYARDS. See also ANCHOR, PAINTER, ROPE, SYNTHETICS.

Care should be taken to check your lines for any signs of wear and tear so that they may be replaced before they break (PART) while you are out on the water. It is a good idea always to carry an extra length or two.

One simple way of protecting that portion of a line that gets a lot of chafing is to encase it in an old piece of split rubber hose—for instance, around the point at which the MOORING line goes through the CHOCK on the bow. Canvas sewn around the line, or a sponge-rubber pad, will also protect it at points of strain. This protection is known as "chafing gear." See Fig. 29.

live ballast You and your crew.

loose-footed sail Sail not attached to anything along its bottom edge but only at each corner.

A DINGHY's one sail is often loose-footed, and a JIB is practically always loose-footed.

lubber line Lengthwise line on a compass bowl which points to the bow.

luff 1. Front edge of a FORE-AND-AFT sail.

This is the spot to keep your eye on when BEATING. If it quivers or flaps, you are not keeping your sail full and will lose headway, so head the bow away from the wind. See BEAT, SAILBOAT PARTS, and Plate 34. 2. To turn the boat toward or into the wind (often with UP). 3. To shake or quiver (of a sail), as the wind is spilled out of the sail with the result that the boat is slowed.

Luffing is accomplished in two ways—with the TILLER and with the sail. You can steer the boat into the wind with the tiller, or you can let out the sail by letting the SHEET run out. By the same token, if you are luffing involuntarily and do not want to be, pull the tiller away from the sail to head the boat away from the wind, or pull the sail in.

Luffing—whether by means of the tiller or the sail —is your "safety valve" if the wind gets too strong and you are afraid of capsizing on a BEAT or a REACH, as in both cases the sail is emptied of its wind (and the boat returns to an even keel). However, the boat also loses its forward motion and is thus harder to control, so don't head into the wind or SLACK OFF the sheets any more or any longer than necessary. Since the beating skipper should be sitting on the side of the boat away from the sail (to WINDWARD), he will push the tiller down toward the sail, away from himself, to head the boat into the wind. On a reach, since it takes longer to head up into the wind, letting the MAINSHEET run out in the puffs may be sufficient, but don't let the end of the boom catch in the water. See HEEL.

Sailing by the luff can be a help when the puffs don't seem to let up or if for some reason a REEF is impractical. Trim the JIB in tight and let the mainsail luff continually, and at the same time don't try to POINT too high, keeping your boat moving (FOOTING).

Whatever else you do, *don't* cleat the mainsheet.

lugger Boat with a lugsail, often with more than one mast.

lugsail Sail hung from a crosspiece which is attached at an angle to the mast.

A boat with a lugsail—for example, the Chinese junk —is lug-rigged.

M

main halyard Rope (LINE) by which the MAINSAIL is hauled up and down.

It is attached to the top (HEAD) of the mainsail by either a simple knot or by some sort of snap or SHACKLE. When the sail has been pulled up, the pulling end is fastened on a CLEAT to the right (STARBOARD) of the mast, either on the deck, on the mast itself, or on the COAMING. See READYING, SAILBOAT PARTS.

mainsail (pronounced "mainsl") Large sail on the back (AFT side) of the mainmast.

It is attached to the mast either by SLIDES running on a TRACK or by insertion of the BOLTROPE along the sail's edge into a groove in the mast. The bottom (FOOT) of the sail is attached to the BOOM, either at its two ends only (a LOOSE-FOOTED sail) or all along its length by sail tracks or groove as on the mast. The third edge (the LEECH), unattached, is stiffened with three or four narrow slats (BATTENS) of varying lengths inserted into pockets in the sail.

The three corners of a MARCONI sail (the most common type) are the HEAD (the top), the TACK (the corner where the boom and the mast meet), and the CLEW (at the outer end of the boom).

Its three sides are the LUFF (next to the mast), the FOOT (next to the boom) and the LEECH (the outer back edge).

The mainsail is pulled up and down by the MAIN HALYARD; once up, it is pulled in and let out (TRIMMED) by the MAINSHEET.

A mainsail may also be of the GAFF type, with four sides and another pole, the gaff, projecting out from the upper part of the mast to hold up the fourth side. The top corner is the PEAK and the corner where the gaff and mast meet is the THROAT. See GAFF, SAILBOAT PARTS.

mainsheet   Rope (LINE) attached to the BOOM by a system of pulleys (BLOCKS) and with which the MAINSAIL is pulled in and let out while the boat is under sail. See SAILBOAT PARTS.

The end of the mainsheet is usually fastened to the end of the boom, then is led down to the block on the TRAVELER, which allows it to slide across from side to side when the sail swings over the boat, then back to one or two blocks both on the underside of the boom. Thus the end of the mainsheet with which you control the sail comes off approximately the middle of the boom and into the COCKPIT. Put a FIGURE EIGHT KNOT in this end so that it cannot run through the block if you should inadvertently let go of it. See Fig. 20.

Before you raise the sail, be sure that the sheet is uncleated and untangled so that the sail will flap freely until you are ready to depart. Never cleat the sheet while you are sailing in a small boat. Either hold it, or if this becomes too tiring in heavy weather, take a half turn under a centrally located cleat (as on the CENTERBOARD TRUNK), or install a quick-release device such as a SNATCH BLOCK or CAM CLEAT. See Figs. 2 and 6.

After you have lowered the mainsail, haul the mainsheet all the way in, cleat it and coil it, laying the coil end-side down on the flooring or seat (CAPSIZE the coil).

And remember—the mainsheet is *not* a sail—it's a rope, or better yet, a LINE.

maintenance   Upkeep, or as Webster says, "sustenance."

Proper care of a sailboat is as important as proper handling and learning to sail correctly. A new sailboat can be ruined in one year or sailed successfully for forty, depending on how it is treated.

Prevention. An "ounce of prevention" and a "stitch in time" are two cardinal rules of boat care. Be good to your boat in your everyday use of it, and you will save yourself hours and dollars of repair and replacement:

See that it does not get scratched or gouged.

Wear rubber soles or go barefoot.

Keep the DINGHY from knocking against it.

Use FENDERS and GUNWALE GUARD whenever possible.

Keep your boat bailed out, but be careful that your bailer does not mar the boat.

Use a COCKPIT cover to lessen both the bailing job and deterioration of paint and varnish or "bright work."

When you remove your RUDDER after sailing, lay it on a cushion to protect the seat (or floorboards) and tie it down to keep it from bouncing around.

Don't let lighted cigarettes, oil, or grease get near your sails; and lower the sails carefully so that they do not get caught—on STAYS, CLEATS, CENTERBOARD TRUNK, etc.; avoid deep creases when you put the sails away.

Tape sharp ends of wire.

WHIP or tape rope ends to prevent fraying; nylon and Dacron lines can be made fray-free by searing them with a match.

And then use your own common sense to add to these "ounces of prevention."

A stitch in time. Quick repair of the first signs of damage or wear is the second maxim of a good skipper: fill and paint scars on the HULL; mend small sail tears; SPLICE or replace frayed ropes and wires. Each sailor will learn to add to the list from his own experience.

Summer care. When it comes to summer care, winter laying-up and spring fitting out, the modern sailor need spend only a fraction of the time once needed, because of the increasing use of fiber glass hulls, aluminum SPARS, stainless steel hardware, and Dacron sails and lines.

However, there will never be a complete end to upkeep, especially for the salt-water sailor. Marine growth develops on all materials—fiber glass is not maintenance-free—and a good scrubbing is in order at least once or twice a summer. Pull your boat out of the water (see CAREEN), put on your bathing suit, get some good stiff brushes, soap, and fresh water, and go to work to remove all the scum, green growth, and barnacles. If it needs it, apply a fresh coat of ANTI-FOULING paint to the bottom.

Winter care. When the fall comes and the boat is hauled out of the water, most small boat sailors are usually able to find a storage spot in their own or a friend's backyard. If you have a trailer, it makes a good winter resting place for the boat; otherwise use saw-horses or some sort of framework, being careful to pad it well so as not to mar the hull. Opinion seems to favor storing the boat right side up in its natural position. Abnormal stresses and strains that might occur if the boat is stored upside down are thus avoided.

Outdoor storage in a protected place and with a good tarpaulin or other covering is adequate, a shed or barn, better. A heated cellar or garage, on the other hand, dries out the paint too much. If yours is a wooden boat, be sure it gets adequate ventilation, or you will run the risk of dry rot. Have an opening at each end of the cover, or throw back the canvas every now and then on a sunny day during the winter.

Remove mast and BOOM, and if they are of wood, store them where they will lie flat and straight. Take out everything else—sails, ropes, GEAR, TILLER, etc. (including the CENTERBOARD if possible)—and see that they are clean, dry, and neat before storing. Remove the drain plug, if there is one. Metal fittings should be given a protective coat of oil or grease (household wax polish for aluminum).

Painting. Some sailors like to get a jump on the work of fitting out in the spring by doing some fall scraping, painting, and varnishing. If you have a wooden boat which needs repainting (as it does at least every year or two, you can use some of the sunny fall days to scrape and sand off the old paint, and get at least one coat on before winter sets in. RUDDER, BOOM, and mast will go through the winter better with a fall coat of varnish.

Fiber glass hulls may not *need* paint, but there are many owners who like to paint their plastic boats after a couple of seasons, for various reasons: to change the color; to freshen up the appearance; to hide repairs, scratches, and faded or streaked places; and to cover up hairline cracks that frequently develop on the fiber glass coating.

Your marine or hardware dealer can help you with advice on preparation and painting of both wood and fiber glass. Ask him about the new epoxy paints which are particularly good for refinishing fiber glass.

Before you know it, spring will come once again and you will be ready to launch your boat. Your gear has all been put back in place and now (if you are on salt water) your last chore is to apply that coat of anti-fouling paint. For wood or fiber glass alike, this is a must, and strange as it may seem, most anti-fouling paints are applied just before the boat is launched so the paint is still wet as the boat goes into the water. (Some new paints are applied differently—read the instructions on the can.)

make fast See FAST.

Marconi rig Tall mast that carries a triangular fore-and-aft MAINSAIL with a fairly short BOOM and has largely replaced the four-sided GAFF RIG; also called a Bermuda or Bermudian rig.

The name comes from the fact that the early Marconi mast was so much taller than the old familiar gaff-rigged mast that it needed many wires and STAYS to support it and so resembled a Marconi wireless tower.

Your CATBOAT or SLOOP will probably have a Mar-

127

coni rig unless it is several years old. See RIG, SAILBOAT PARTS.

marina Dock or boat basin.

marline (pronounced "marl'n") Small two-strand rope.

marlinespike Wooden or metal pointed instrument used to open a strand of rope.

"Marlinespike Seamanship" is often the title of a chapter in books on how to sail—and includes knots, knot tying, splicing, whipping, etc. However, on the small boat of today, a few simple knots will do almost everything you need; most of the synthetic ropes do not need whipping; and the sailor's palm is not as normal a part of the equipment as it used to be. See KNOT, SPLICE, WHIP.

marry To join two ropes. See SPLICE.

mast Upright pole (SPAR) to which a sail is attached. See SAILBOAT PARTS.

There are many factors which determine what is the best mast for a boat: wood vs. aluminum, groove vs. track, thickness of the wall, weight, diameter, and the whole system of supports. The choice of the best mast for a particular boat is such a technical matter that the new sailor must trust that the boatbuilder has chosen the best combination of specifications for his mast or that the class association knows what it is doing.

In many small boats the mast is movable as well as removable. It can be lifted in and out for ease in travel and for DRY SAILING and to transform the boat into a rowboat or outboard motorboat. When there are two mast holes in the bow of a small boat—one behind the other—the boat can be rigged either as a CATBOAT (with the mast well forward and only one sail) or as a SLOOP (mast farther back so that a JIB can be added in front of the mast). See CATBOAT, RIG, SLOOP, and Plate 54.

When the mast has been put in place (STEPPED), it must be TUNED, by adjusting the supports, the slant (or RAKE—see Fig. 27), the tightness of the wire supports

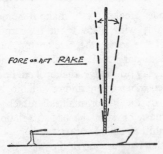

Figure 27. Rake of Mast

(STAYS and SHROUDS). See Plates 6 and 7. The mast of a small boat should in general be straight up and down (although some racing boats have curves, bows, etc.), with the stays and shrouds at the sides and front tightened so they are not slack. (When you sail, the LEEWARD shroud will be slack and the WINDWARD one tight.) Some masts are also supported by permanent BACKSTAYS or RUNNING BACKSTAYS (RUNNERS). The latter must be tightened and loosened alternately each time the sail changes sides.

Two methods are widely used to attach the MAINSAIL to the mast: a groove in the mast into which the edge (LUFF) of the sail is inserted by means of a BOLTROPE, or a succession of SLIDES sewed into the luff of the sail which fit on a TRACK on the mast. See Fig. 28 for three types of mast cross sections.

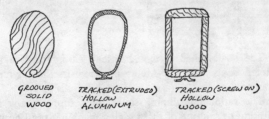

GROOVED SOLID WOOD TRACKED (EXTRUDED) HOLLOW ALUMINUM TRACKED (SCREW ON) HOLLOW WOOD

Figure 28. Mast Sections

129

If your mast breaks, try to make it home as best you can (preferably with a tow) but be careful not to let either end of the mast (the broken top part or the un-stepped bottom part) poke a hole in or injure the boat in any way. Try to wedge the broken bottom part se-curely with cushions or anything available, and sail home with a part of the jib or mainsail attached to what is left of the mast, or even the BOOM, set up in its place. (This makeshift is called a JURY RIG.)

mast cap Fitting over the top of the mast. See Fig. 41.

masthead Top of the mast.

meter class One of the several classes of boats that con-form to the International Class Meter Rule.

Meter class boats, like ONE-DESIGN CLASS BOATS, race against each other without handicap; but unlike one-design boats, are similar but not identical in their design. Whereas one-design class boat racing tests only sailing skill, meter class boat racing also provides for testing design ingenuity. The International Class Meter Rule is a complicated formula that permits, within compensating limits, variations in sail area, length, displacement, draft, freeboard, and beam. Thus any of these specifications may vary. The approximate lengths of the leading meter classes are:

Meter Class	Overall Length (in feet)	Waterline Length (in feet)
12	70	46
10	60	38
8	50	32
6	40	25
5.5	35	23

The boats sailed in the America's Cup races are 12-Meter boats. The 5.5-Meter is raced in the Olympic Games.

The rational beginning sailor must suppress any as-piration to sail one of these racing machines until he has had lots of sailing experience! At the same time he may console himself with the thought that the racers in these beauties are only doing the same things he does in his sailing DINGHY.

midships Same as AMIDSHIPS.

miss stays To be unable to GO ABOUT; to get into irons, or stays. See IN IRONS.

miter To cut on an angle, as a sail is *miter cut*.

mizzen Sail on the MIZZENMAST, the mast farthest toward the stern on a two-masted boat, especially a YAWL or a KETCH. See RIG.

mizzenmast Small mast behind (AFT of) the mainmast on a YAWL or a KETCH; a jigger.

The main difference between a yawl and a ketch lies in the placement of the mizzenmast: on a yawl it is aft of the steering mechanism and on a ketch it is in front (FORWARD) of the rudder or wheel. See RIG.

moor To tie (make fast) a boat to a mooring or dock.

mooring Permanent combination of anchor, chain, buoy, etc., to which a boat is attached (moored) to keep it in one place, free-floating on the water.

Your mooring should be as handy to you and your DINGHY as possible, and still be in a sheltered spot and placed to allow your boat to swing freely without bumping your neighbor's boat, no matter which way the wind blows.

Although the ideal mooring calls for a total overall length (SCOPE) of five to nine times the height of the water at its highest tide, in today's crowded anchorages this may not always be possible. Use of an ample anchor, and a heavy chain plus a light chain has allowed for reduction in this formula. One formula for a sailboat up to 25 feet consists of the following (See Fig. 29): (1) A MUSHROOM anchor (75–125 lbs.), (2) A heavy chain ($\frac{3}{8}''$–$\frac{5}{8}''$) one and a half times as long as the maximum water depth, attached by a swivel SHACKLE to (3) A light chain ($\frac{3}{16}''$–$\frac{5}{16}''$) the same length as high

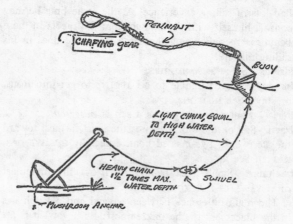

Figure 29. Mooring

water depth, which runs up to a (4) Hollow metal
or plastic buoy, and (5) A rope (PENNANT), ½″–¾″
manila or ½″ nylon, about the length of the boat,
attached to the buoy and leading to the boat. Many
moorings have only the heavy chain and then heavy
rope, but in this case the full scope should be greater
than the above. Find out about local customs, conditions,
or even rules before you buy your GROUND TACKLE
and then probably you would do well to buy the whole
mooring complete.

Morse code Signaling system in which letters and numerals are represented by different combinations of dots
and dashes.

It may be used either visually with flashing light signals or audibly with sound signals. In both cases the
duration of the dash is three times that of the dot. See
DISTRESS SIGNAL, SIGNALING.

mouse 1. Yarn or material wound around a STAY or a
rope to keep a loop from slipping past it. 2. To make

such a device as in **1**. **3.** To wrap rope or material around a hook to keep it from coming unfastened.

mushroom Type of anchor used for a mooring, with a long shank and round convex bottom that digs farther into a soft ocean bottom the longer it is left there. See MOORING.

N

nautical mile 6080 feet—thus a mile over water is farther than over land (5280 feet).

navigating lights Required lights at sea. See LIGHTS.

navigation Art or science of safely conducting a boat from place to place.

Although the small boat sailor need not be an expert navigator, his pleasure in sailing can be greatly enhanced and he can safely venture farther out to enjoy the delights of cruising if he knows something about simple navigation. His needs are: charts of the waters he will be in, a compass, a pair of dividers, and a straightedge course protractor. See BEARING, CHART, COMPASS, COMPASS ROSE, FIX, PILOTING.

navigational aid Device or apparatus to help the skipper determine his ship's course, either on board his boat (chart, compass calculations, etc.) or outside the boat (buoys, lighthouses, landmarks, stars, etc.). See BUOY, CHART.

nun, nun buoy See BUOY.

O

oakum Old, tarred rope strands used for stuffing into openings between boards of HULL to prevent leaking.

oar Pole with a handle at one end and a broad blade at the other, used in pairs to propel a boat.

Your sailboat should be equipped with at least one oar (or paddle) in case you are becalmed, lose your RUDDER or sail, or break your BOOM.

oarlock Horned or pronged device, one on each rim (GUNWALE) of a small boat to hold oars in place while pulling; a rowlock.

An oarlock mounted on the back (TRANSOM) of the boat is a "sculling lock."

occulting Disappearing and reappearing, used of a navigational light at sea; an occulting light is a recurring light with longer periods of light than of darkness, a steady light totally eclipsed at intervals.

off To seaward of; outside of; away from, as the wind is *off shore*, or the lighthouse is *off the starboard beam*. See DIRECTION.

off the wind Away from the direction of the wind; not CLOSE-HAULED into the wind; opposite of ON THE WIND; hence REACHING or RUNNING.

If you are sailing on the wind and want to sail off the wind, pull the TILLER away from the side the sail is on and let out (EASE) the sheets. You will thus go from a close-hauled position to a CLOSE reach, then on to a BEAM reach, to a BROAD reach, and finally to a run with the wind behind you: all of which are positions off the wind.

on board On the boat; aboard.

one-design class boat Boat built to uniform specifications and measurements so that it is comparable to all the other boats in that class for competitive purposes.

The sail usually carries the insignia or initials of the class and a number, every boat in the class being assigned a number as it is built (thus a low number denotes an older boat); each class organization holds local, national, and even international competitions, checks boat measurements, and often publishes a magazine.

There are literally hundreds of different kinds of one-design boats, such as the Snipe, Lightning, Comet, Star, Penguin, Blue Jay, Quad, and Scow. The Snipe class led in numbers in 1961, there having been some 13,500 of them registered throughout the world since 1931.

Although some boat manufacturers advertise their boats as "one-design" because these boats are all identical, it should be recognized that this does not necessarily mean that they are one-design class boats. In order for a boat to qualify as a class boat, its complete specifications must be available to all builders and production may not be restricted to a single manufacturer. Write to Sailing Secretary, National Association of Engine and Boat Manufacturers, 420 Lexington Avenue, New York 17, for a booklet on one-design sailboats. See METER CLASS.

on the beam Lying outside and at right angles to the boat, 90° from the direction of the bow on either the STARBOARD or PORT side. See DIRECTION.

on the bow Lying outside and off the bow of the boat in a 90° sector extending 45° on either side of the bow. See DIRECTION.

on the quarter Lying outside and off the stern of the boat in a 90° sector extending 45° on either side of the stern. See DIRECTION.

on the wind Sailing CLOSE-HAULED toward the wind's direction; beating; sailing by the wind; sailing to WINDWARD; tacking; opposite of OFF THE WIND.

outboard 1. Outside the HULL. 2. Outboard motor, i.e., a portable motor fastened over the stern of a boat. See Plate 51.

outfoot To go faster than another boat. See FOOT.

outhaul Small LINE (or fitting, such as a SHACKLE) fastened to the lower back corner (CLEW) of a sail to stretch it along the BOOM, and attached at the end of the boom. See READYING, SAILBOAT PARTS.

outpoint To sail closer into the wind than another boat. See POINT.

over Same as HARD-ALEE.

overboard Outside the boat, over the side.

"Man overboard" needs not definition, but immediate action. Even though the person is a good swimmer, toss him a life preserver, aiming beside him rather than at him. Then turn around, going DOWNWIND of him so that you can turn back into the wind to come up slowly beside him, just as you do in making a LANDING, (or you may JIBE if it seems best). If you have to go in after him, first tie one end of a rope to yourself and the other end to the boat. See Fig. 30.

If you yourself fall overboard while sailing alone, don't try to swim back to your boat until you have stopped to watch it long enough to figure out its sailing pattern, which will be a series of half circles.

overhand knot See KNOT.

overhand loop See KNOT.

overhaul 1. To go over RIGGING carefully to see that all is clear. 2. To overtake another boat. 3. To renovate a vessel.

overstand To go too far in aiming for a specific goal,

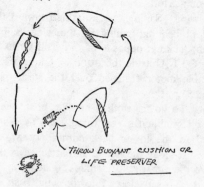

ROUND UP INTO WIND AND
COAST TO MAN.

THROW BUOYANT CUSHION OR
LIFE PRESERVER

Figure 30. Man Overboard

especially in BEATING to reach a point directly into the wind.

When TACKING up to an object (like a BUOY) directly in the direction of the wind, in a series of zigzags, you try to have the object at right angles to your boat as you COME ABOUT so that you will just be able to reach it on that last tack (and if need be, allowing for tide and current). If you do not quite make it, you will have to come about still another time. On the other hand, you may go farther than necessary and find that you have *overstood* the mark—probably less serious in time lost than in not going far enough, but even so a miscalculation for a racer. See TACK.

overtake   To catch up with and pass another boat; to overhaul.

The RULES OF THE ROAD always require that the over-taking boat must watch out for the boat being overtaken, regardless of method of propulsion. See RIGHT OF WAY.

140

P

pad Metal eye fastened on a flat surface, as on a deck.

paddle 1. Short pole with a flat oarlike end and a flared handle used to propel a canoe.

Always take a paddle (or an oar) in your sailboat in case you are becalmed, lose your RUDDER or sail, or need to use it as a "splint" for a broken BOOM. 2. To propel a boat with a paddle.

painter Rope on the bow of a boat for making fast to a dock or MOORING.

parachute, parachute spinnaker Correct name for the modern spinnaker with interchangeable and identical LUFF and LEECH; a double spinnaker; a kite. See SPIN-NAKER.

parrel Rope which holds JAWS of a GAFF to the mast.

part To break, said of a rope.

partner Strengthening board to help support something set through an opening in the deck, such as a mast or BITT. (Usually used in plural.)

pay off, pay away To head away from the wind; to fall off.

pay out To slacken or let out a rope or a chain; to ease; to start.

To pay out usually connotes letting out the rope some distance, while to START or EASE a rope is more often to loosen it only a small amount.

peak 1. Highest corner of a quadrilateral or GAFF-RIG sail. 2. Upper end of the gaff. See Fig. 12.

peak halyard Rope which hoists the PEAK. See Fig. 12.

pennant, pendant 1. Long, narrow, three-cornered flag.

2. Short rope, usually with a metal eye (THIMBLE) in the end, as the *mooring pennant* (see Fig. 29) or the *centerboard pennant*.

pile Pole, as for a dock, driven into the sea bottom and projecting above the water to hold up a dock or pier.

piling Structure of PILES.

piloting That part of NAVIGATION related to conducting a boat through channels, harbors, and along a coast using aids to navigation to fix one's position.

Piloting involves watching the depth of the water, tides and currents, knowledge of the RULES OF THE ROAD, whistle signals, lights for various types of craft, fog signals, buoyage and lighthouse systems, and safety equipment to have aboard.

The small boat sailor aspiring to be a big boat sailor should undertake to learn piloting. A common and pleasant way to learn is to take a piloting course given by a local chapter of the U. S. Power Squadron or the Coast Guard Auxiliary. See COMPASS, NAVIGATION.

pinch When sailing into the wind (BEATING), to pull the sail in too tight or head the bow of the boat into the wind too much, so that the sail begins to shiver (LUFF) and the boat becomes sluggish and does not FOOT well. See BEAT.

pintle Pin over which an eye or socket (the gudgeon) fits. See GUDGEON, RUDDER.

plane To go through the water with the bow up and out, above the waves, and at a faster speed than your usual one.

The exhilarating art of planing is not for the novice, as it takes both skill and a fairly stiff breeze. It is a matter of that quick extra fillip on the TILLER and SHEET at just the right moment to get the boat riding up on top of the bow wave. In order to get your boat to plane: (1) You should be on a REACH, (2) Have a fairly flat-bottomed boat, (3) Get your boat level by vigorous HIKING-OUT, (4) When the puff comes, FALL OFF rather than LUFF UP, (5) Give a quick pull on the MAINSHEET, and away you jump.

Boats that can be coaxed to plane include International 14s, 5-0-5s, Thistles, and Scows.

plastic Capable of being molded, as FIBER GLASS.

The use of plastics has, and will continue to have, great impact on the small boat industry. Tough and durable fiber glass has replaced wood to an increasing extent over the last decade, and new materials are constantly being tried. See CHOOSING A BOAT, MAINTENANCE.

plug Stopper in drain hole of a boat.

Take it out when you put up your boat for the winter, but don't forget it in the spring!

pocket 1. Curving bulge in the sail near the mast; belly. 2. Long, thin double thickness of cloth into which a BATTEN is inserted, usually at three points along the outer edge (LEECH) of the MAINSAIL; batten pocket. See BATTEN, READYING, SAILBOAT PARTS.

point 1. Place or mark on the shore or water to use in finding direction or holding course; as in REACHING, one sails for a point, rather than according to the LUFF of the sail. 2. One of the thirty-two divisions of the compass; North, South, East, West are the four cardinal points, and the intercardinals, North-northeast, Northeast, etc., are the points in between, each $11\frac{1}{4}°$ apart. See COMPASS. 3. To ornament the end of a rope. 4. To sail as close to the wind as possible without letting the mainsail shiver (LUFF); also *point up* or *point high*.

points of sailing Direction of boat in relation to the wind.

The three basic points of sailing are:

RUNNING—when the wind is from behind (ASTERN).

REACHING—when the wind is to the side (ABEAM).

BEATING—when the wind is ahead (ON THE BOW).

Your boat depends on a force outside it—the wind—to give it life and movement, and this force can come from only one direction at a given time. Therefore your ability to make the boat go where you want it to go depends on how you harness this power. You can go anywhere you like with wind (though not always in a straight line), by working the sails and the RUDDER in relation to the wind's direction. If you want to go in the same direction as the wind, it will blow you there from astern (as in the old days of the square-riggers when a following wind was a necessity), but even if your objective is not in the direction toward which the wind is blowing, you can regulate sails and steering so as to attain your goal. And for each change in your boat's direction, there must always be a change in the TRIM of the sails. This is perhaps best shown on a clocklike circle of ten possible points of sailing: beating on both PORT and STARBOARD TACKS, reaching (CLOSE, BEAM, and BROAD) on both tacks, and running on both tacks. See Fig. 31.

For regulating your boat in relation to the three basic points of sailing, see RUN (wind behind), REACH (wind to the side), BEAT (wind in front).

For pulling in or letting out your sails to fit the changes in direction, see TRIM.

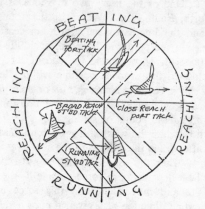

Figure 31. Points of Sailing

poop 1. Raised part of afterdeck on a ship. 2. To have a wave come in over the stern when RUNNING (usually in passive—a boat is *pooped* when the sea comes in over the stern).

port 1. The left side of a boat when facing forward (formerly LARBOARD); the opposite of STARBOARD. See DIRECTION. 2. Safe place for boats; a harbor. 3. Window in a ship's side.

port tack Sailing with the wind coming over the left (PORT) side, while the sail is on the right (STARBOARD) side. See Plate 21.

A boat on the port tack must get out of the way of a boat on the starboard tack. See BEAT, RIGHT OF WAY, TACK.

power squadron See U. S. POWER SQUADRON.

pram 1. Flat-bottomed Dutch or Norwegian boat. 2. Small DINGHY with a cutoff or semicircular bow.

privileged Having the RIGHT OF WAY; opposite of BUR-DENED.

Under the RULES OF THE ROAD a boat CLOSE-HAULED on the PORT tack must keep out of the way of a boat on the STARBOARD tack and the latter is the privileged boat. See RIGHT OF WAY.

pulley Wheel with a groove in its rim in which a rope or chain is passed.

Landlubbers err doubly when calling a BLOCK a pulley. Technically a pulley is the non-nautical equivalent of a SHEAVE, the grooved wheel, and the sheave is but one of the several parts of a block.

put about Cause (the boat) to COME ABOUT, 90° on the other TACK; to come about; to go about.

145

Q

quarter That part of a boat's side between the midpoint (BEAM) or 90°, and the stern, or 180°. See DIRECTION.

quartering Coming from a point back of the middle (the BEAM) and not directly ASTERN of a boat; coming over the QUARTER, said of wind or waves; also, sailing with the wind coming over the quarter.

R

racing Competitive sailing.

Racing is a sport unto itself which this book does not attempt to cover. Your library will have books on sailboat racing. The rules are detailed and specific and may be obtained from the North American Yacht Racing Union, 37 West 44th Street, New York 36, New York.

There is a difference of opinion among sailing instructors as to whether to schedule races for beginners, and so teach sailing through racing. We would not agree that learning through competition is as sound as acquiring the fundamentals first, straight and unadorned. Sailing can be exciting and varied enough without the necessity for extra stimulus. However, the basics need not take long for a group of eager learners, and an informal racing program could certainly be included in the "intermediate" class.

rail Board or railing along the top of the BULWARK, or at the outer edge of the deck.

rake Slant of a mast, either forward or backward, from the perpendicular. See MAST.

range **1.** Difference between high and low tide. **2.** Direction line in navigating, as a steeple is *in range* with a water tank. See COMPASS.

rap full Sailing with all sails filled with wind.

rattail Tapered end of a rope, such as the end of a BOLT-ROPE in the edge of a sail.

reach **1.** Sailing course in which the wind blows against the side of the boat (the wind is ABEAM); any course between (and except) a BEAT to WINDWARD (CLOSE-HAULED into the wind) and a RUN (the wind behind you and the sails all the way out). **2.** To sail with the wind coming from the side (ABEAM) and the sail neither all the way in nor all the way out; to sail on a reach. See POINTS OF SAILING, Plate 23.

Since reaching covers a wide range of sailing positions, it is broken down into three different kinds of reaches, depending upon the relation between boat and wind: a *close reach,* a *beam reach* and a *broad reach.* See Fig. 32.

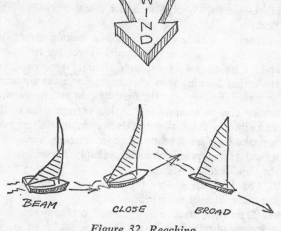

Figure 32. Reaching

A *close reach* is a course with the boat somewhat farther away from the direction of the wind than when beating completely close-hauled. The SHEETS are not quite pulled all the way in, but EASED a little. With shifts in the wind, a beat can become a close reach and vice versa.

A *beam reach* is a course with the wind broadside

and the sails and BOOM halfway between close-hauled for beating and all the way out for running.

A *broad reach* is a course with the wind nearer the stern than abeam, and the sails let out beyond a 45° angle but not as far out as for running. The wind is ABAFT the BEAM or ON THE QUARTER. See DIRECTION.

Because reaching is the easiest and safest as well as one of the fastest ways to sail, it is recommended as a good way to start off—also because you can reach away from your MOORING with the sail on one side for a time and then reach back in approximately the same amount of time with the sail on the other side. This may seem like a trivial point, but it is all too easy to sail away happily running straight before the wind for half the afternoon, and then turn back, not realizing that on the return trip you must sail in a zigzag course against the wind (TACKING and BEATING). This, of course, will take many times as long as the quick ride out with the wind behind you. So start off on a reach with the wind blowing at right angles to the boat on the right side, a STARBOARD beam reach, then COME ABOUT and return on a PORT beam reach.

When reaching, you are sailing or steering for a definite point (a landmark on the shore or a BUOY), as opposed to beating, when you must sail as close into the wind as possible (since your goal is directly in the direction of the wind and you cannot point your boat toward it). The sails must be kept full—as always—but by pulling them in and letting them out (TRIMMING them) to meet the shifts in the wind rather than by changing the boat's direction with the TILLER.

This means that the skipper chooses a point on the shore, keeps his boat headed for it in as straight a line as he can, and the crew works the sails, at first letting them out (STARTING or EASING them) till they wrinkle or flutter (LUFF) just a bit, and then trimming them in so that they are full, and keeps them in this relative position vis-à-vis the wind by testing the luff now and then. If the sails are trimmed in too far, the boat will not sail as well or as fast as it should, you may tip (HEEL) more than necessary and may even run the risk of capsizing. If they are out too far, they will flutter and you will slow down. The CENTERBOARD should be about halfway down on a beam reach.

The close reach is similar to the beam reach described above except that the boom and the sails are trimmed in a bit more and the centerboard is lowered; on a broad reach the sheets are eased more than on the beam reach and the centerboard is up somewhat more since you are nearer a run.

Do not come about from a reach directly, but trim in your sails to the close-hauled position first, pushing the tiller slowly toward the sail as you do so, and then go about. See COME ABOUT.

reaching jib Large JIB used usually in racing when on a BROAD REACH, one of the LIGHT SAILS.

ready about Skipper's command to warn the crew and passengers that he is going to turn the bow of the boat into the wind so that the BOOM and sail swing across the boat, and go on the other TACK.

The crew's responsibility is to get ready to change JIB SHEETS, BACKSTAYS, weight, etc. See COME ABOUT.

readying Getting ready to go sailing.

Getting the boat ready for sailing involves the various steps preparatory to CASTING OFF, after you have once gotten to your sailboat (for getting to a boat at its MOORING, see DINGHY). These steps include:

(1) Noting the direction of the wind as you come aboard. (If at a mooring and there is no current, the way your boat swings will show you the wind's direction. See WIND.) (2) Removing canvas cover. (3) Stowing GEAR, checking equipment. (4) Bailing and sponging boat dry (see Plates 56, 57). (5) Lowering CENTERBOARD or DAGGERBOARD (see Plate 9). (6) Putting on

RUDDER and TILLER. (7) Putting on, or BENDING, the sails, including insertion of BATTENS, removal of BOOM CRUTCH. (8) Hoisting sails and CLEATING ropes (LINES).

Whether your boat is kept close by, tied to a dock in front of the house, moored some distance away, or brought many miles on a trailer, you will probably keep some equipment in it (like battens and DITTY BAG) and will also be bringing some along with you (like sails, life jacket, sweater, paddle and bailer. See GEAR).

If your boat has a canvas cover stretched over the COCKPIT to keep out the rain, unfasten and roll it up, starting at the stern, and stow it on the dock or in the dinghy if you are cramped for space; you won't need it and it could get wet and messy while you are out.

Be sure you and your crew and guests have on rubber- or soft-soled shoes. Your deck and floorboards will need enough TLC anyway without heel marks and holes.

Store your gear neatly away under the bow or stern deck and seats, check over your lines, STAYS, SHROUDS and "hardware" for any damage or weak spots, and get your boat dry (most boats have removable floorboards for ease of bailing).

Lowering the centerboard or inserting the daggerboard will be necessary sooner or later, so you may as well do it now since this will give you a bit more stability as you climb around in the boat.

Now is also a good time to put on the rudder and tiller, either separately or in combination (or if they have been left in place, untie the tiller). Various devices such as a socket and pin (called GUDGEON and PINTLE), or a heavy piece of TRACK, are used to fasten the rudder to the stern of the boat. Be sure to get the tiller under the wire (TRAVELER) that stretches across the back part of the deck for the MAINSHEET's pulley (BLOCK).

Now for the sail or sails. First, always be sure your bow is facing the wind. Bending on the sails at first seems rather overwhelming, as yard upon yard of white Dacron keeps flowing out of the sail bag. In addition to spreading them out beforehand at home in order to become familiar with their shapes and sizes, some people like to mark the corners for faster recognition. But you will soon learn to note such signs as these: a row of SNAP HOOKS means the front edge (LUFF) of the JIB (always put it into the bag last—unless it has its own—then it is first out); a pointed board sewn inside the cloth is the head of the MAINSAIL; the corner of the sail with SLIDES running away from it in both directions is the bottom front corner (TACK) of the mainsail, fitting next to both the mast and the BOOM.

Begin with the jib (unless you are in a CATBOAT), which is fastened at its three corners and all along its luff. Follow these steps (see Fig. 33):

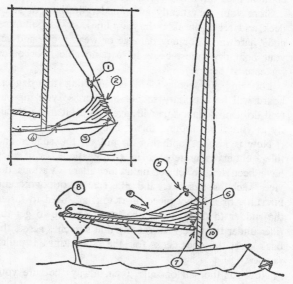

Figure 33. Readying

(1) Unfasten (from its CLEAT or other safe place near the foot of the mast) the rope (JIB HALYARD) with which you pull up the jib, and look up along its length to be sure it is not twisted or caught, taking care *not* to let go of it. Attach this jib halyard to the top of the jib by knot, snap hook, or SHACKLE.

(2) Attach the snap hooks (or other fasteners) along the luff of the sail to the wire that goes from the mast to the bow (the JIBSTAY). See Plate 17.

(3) Fasten the lower front corner of the jib to its device on the foremost part of the deck at the bottom of the jibstay.

(4) Fasten the back corner of the jib (the CLEW) to the JIB SHEET fitting which has the two ropes attached to it (jib sheets) by which you manage the jib. These should then be run back through eyeholes (FAIRLEADS—see Plate 19) on the two sides of the deck (one for the PORT TACK and one for the STARBOARD TACK) to their cleats but left uncleated and free. Do not raise the jib now; the mainsail is always raised first.

Now the triangular mainsail—usually attached to both mast and boom by slides along a track or by grooves in the SPARS into which is slid the rope sewn inside the edges of the sail. Your experience with the jib will help you on the mainsail. If you have a GAFF RIG or four-sided sail, see GAFF.

(5) Unfasten the rope that hoists the mainsail (the MAIN HALYARD) from its at-the-mooring resting place, and attach it to the head of the mainsail (and since it is even harder to retrieve this longer halyard, don't inadvertently pull the other end of it before it is made fast to the sail).

(6) Then push the slides (starting with the one at the head of the sail) up the track on the mast, holding them there by a slide stopper of some sort—if none is supplied, make your own by tying a small piece of rope around the mast—until you are ready to hoist sail. If your mast

has a groove instead of a sail track, inserting the edge of the sail and hoisting it must be done together. See Plate 11.

(7) Attach the lower corner of the mainsail next to the mast to the GOOSENECK on the mast (again, devices range from a small rope to a spring shackle).

(8) Now, if the bottom (FOOT) of your sail has no slides or stiffened rope (BOLTROPE) along it, it is LOOSE-FOOTED and attached only at the two ends, not along its foot. You have already attached the end nearest the mast (step No. 7); now fasten the outer end to the end of the boom by the OUTHAUL. If, on the other hand, there are slides or a boltrope in the foot of the sail, start next to the mast with the clew and push the sail along to the outhaul. This is a rope or a device which allows you to adjust the tightness of the sail along the boom—pull it so that there are no wrinkles along the foot of the sail. (If you have a cotton sail, loosen the outhaul if the sail gets wet, so as not to stretch it out of shape.)

(9) Insert the battens (unless they are permanently there) into their POCKETS on the outer edge (the LEECH) of the mainsail (they are held in either by small ropes, snaps, or specially designed pocket-tops).

(10) Before you raise the sails, be sure that the jib sheets and mainsheet are not tangled, knotted, or cleated in any way so that as the sails are pulled up they can "flap" freely, with the boat headed into the wind. Otherwise the boat will sail around, straining its anchor or bumping the other boats at the dock. See Plate 13.

Now take out the boom crutch and hoist away, mainsail first (since this keeps your boat headed into the wind). If something sticks or gets caught, don't force it. Let the sail down a bit, try to see where the trouble lies, and begin again. Watch out for the boom when you get the mainsail up—the flapping sail may cause it to hit you in the head.

Unless your boat is a small dinghy, you will probably

want to ensure that your mainsail is up good and tight by SWAYING or SWEATING UP on the halyard: while one person holds the halyard around a cleat, the other stands on the deck facing the stern and pulls the rope toward him as his colleague quickly takes up this slack around the cleat. Pull the DOWNHAUL on the boom down and fasten it so that the edge of the sail nearest the mast is wrinkle-free or just beginning to show lengthwise wrinkles some inches away from the mast.

Fasten the two halyards on their respective cleats on the forward part of the COCKPIT or on the mast (jib halyard on the left, mainsail halyard on the right) and coil the ropes. To coil, start next to the cleat and run an arm-length of rope through your right hand before you loop it around and grasp it in your left (repeat till rope is all coiled). Now with the coil in your left hand put your right hand through the coil, take hold of the rope between coil and cleat, pull it back out again through the coil toward you, twist it, and "hang up" the coil by putting this loop over the cleat. See Plates 14, 15, 16. Then when you come to let down the sail, just lift the loop off the cleat, lay the coil on the floorboards end side down (CAPSIZE the coil), and the rope runs out freely. (For taking down the sails and "putting the boat to bed" after your sail, see SHIPSHAPE.)

ready to jibe Skipper's command to warn the crew and passengers that he is preparing to JIBE.

reckoning Calculation of a boat's position.

reef 1. Chain of rocks or coral lying submerged near the surface of the water. 2. That part of the sail which is tucked in by reefing. 3. To make the sail area smaller in case of a strong wind. See HEAVY WEATHER.

You should not hesitate to *take a reef* if you find you have to keep LUFFING UP or EASING the MAINSHEET or if you are continually HEELING so that the LEEWARD deck is under water. It is easier to take a reef before you get out on the water—so if there are some white caps or if the boats already out seem to be having rough going, take a reef!

This is done by taking one, two, or even three tucks in the sail along the BOOM (in the FOOT of the sail). The three most common ways to take a reef are: (a) by means of pairs of small ropes (REEF POINTS) sewn permanently in rows on both sides of the lower part of the sail, (b) by means of a rope laced through a permanent row of holes (GROMMETS) in the lower part of the sail, or, (c) by ROLLER REEFING.

The last is the simplest method, since reefing can be accomplished without even lowering the sail, by merely rotating the boom with a cranking device so that the sail is wrapped around the boom and thus made smaller.

When reefing by the other two methods, drop (or raise, if you are still in port) the sail so that the reef points or grommets are just above the boom. Then,

(1) Lash the two ends of the sail by ropes through the CRINGLES, at the TACK and CLEW, pulling the temporary OUTHAUL taut and tying down the extra sail.

(2) Make a neat tight roll of sail and fasten it either by square knots (see KNOT) tied around the roll with the pairs of reef points, or by a spiral lacing through the grommets with a long rope. (An alternative to the latter method is to cut several small ropes to use like reef points through the grommets.)

(3) Tie (or lace) your reefing ropes only around the tucked-in part of the sail (the BUNT), *not* around the boom. See Fig. 34.

In a heavier wind, further reefing can be made in like manner with the second or even the third row of reef points.

Although jibs are not usually reefed (some boats may even carry a substitute "storm jib"), self-furling jibs that can be reduced by any desired amount are now on the market.

When you undo (shake out) the reef, lower the sail

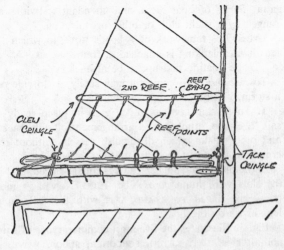

Figure 34. Reef

first, and then be sure all the reef points and lines are free before you hoist sail again. If you should take out your reef while under way, be sure to start at the middle and work toward both ends, releasing the LEECH EARING last.

Because the reduced size of the mainsail gives comparatively more sail power to the jib, reefing often results in too strong a LEE HELM. In this case a smaller jib or no jib at all is the remedy. See WEATHER HELM.

reef band Strip of canvas sewn across sail to strengthen GROMMETS used in reefing. See Fig. 34.

reef knot Same as square knot. See KNOT.

reef point Small rope sewn in both sides of the lower part of a sail and used for taking a reef; they are placed several inches apart in one, two, or three horizontal lines a foot or two above the BOOM. See REEF.

reeve To pass the end of a rope through a BLOCK or a hole.

regatta Series of boat races, and attendant festivities arranged by a yacht club or other organization.

rib Crosswise framework of a boat's HULL to which the lengthwise planking is attached; a frame.

ride To be floating tied up; to be at anchor.

To *ride out* is to come through safely, as to ride out a storm, whether or not at anchor.

rig 1. To fit sails, LINES, STAYS, etc., in place ready to sail. 2. Shape, number, and arrangement of sails, masts, and other SPARS which distinguish vessels, without reference to their HULLS.

In the old days sailing ships were square-rigged, that is, the sails were hung *across* the HULL. Nowadays most boats are rigged FORE AND AFT, with the sails hung lengthwise on the boat.

Fig. 35 illustrates the five most common types of fore-and-aft rigs: CAT, KETCH, SCHOONER, SLOOP, YAWL. A boat with but one sail is a catboat; with a second sail (a JIB), but still only one mast, it is a sloop. A CUTTER differs from a sloop in that it has additional sails (STAY-SAILS, etc.), usually a BOWSPRIT, and carries its mast farther AFT.

A boat with two masts is a schooner, ketch, or yawl. If the two masts are equal in height or the aftermast is taller, it is a schooner. (Boats with more than two masts are types of schooners.) The ketch and yawl differ from the schooner in that the main, or taller, mast is forward of the shorter or MIZZENMAST. The position of the mizzenmast distinguishes the ketch from the yawl. If the mizzenmast is forward of the TILLER, it is a ketch; if it is aft of the tiller, it is a yawl.

The *shape* of the sails also affects the rig of a boat. The most widely used sail shape today is the triangle as exemplified by the MARCONI or JIB-HEADED sail, although there are also many four-sided or GAFF-RIGGED sails still in use. A catboat, sloop, or other type of boat may be outfitted with either three- or four-sided sails.

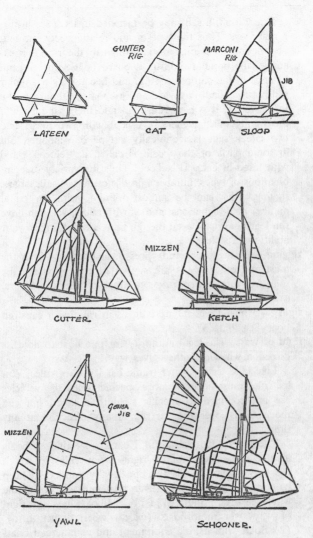

Figure 35. Rig

In addition, a sail may be fastened to its spars in different ways. Thus the type of and relation between gaff, BOOM, and mast may also distinguish the rig. For example, the popular Sailfish, a board boat with one sail, belongs in the catboat family, and because its triangular sail is suspended on a yard and a boom (without a LUFF in between), it is a LATEEN sail and the boat falls into the family of "lateeners." A boat with two masts and two lateen sails is technically a type of schooner, but in some parts of the world is called a "felucca," and with three of each a "xebec"! Thus the variety of combinations of types, number and disposition of sails, spars, rigging, etc., can be almost infinite, with an equal number of designations; and as with knots, you can have fun learning them, even though they add nothing to your ability as a sailor.

rigging All the ropes and wires on a boat by which the mast and other SPARS are supported and by which the sails are worked. See RUNNING RIGGING, SAILBOAT PARTS, STANDING RIGGING.

right To turn (a boat) upright, as in *righting* a capsized boat. See Plate 37.

right of way The legal authority for one boat to hold its direction while the other gives way.

Like land traffic, water traffic has its set of rules. Water rules must be even more specific, since the vehicles are not confined to specific roads and lanes, but can move freely over the surface in any direction at any time.

The general RULES OF THE ROAD for all kinds of boats include these basic sailing right-of-way rules in which the PRIVILEGED boat is the one legally entitled to keep its course, while the BURDENED boat must get out of the way (see Figs. 36 and 37): (1) Sailboats have the right of way over motorboats (except when OVERTAKING). (2) Boats with fishing equipment and commercial boats have the right of way over other boats (except when

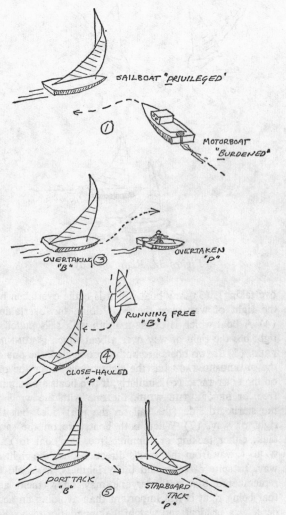

SAILBOAT *PRIVILEGED*

MOTORBOAT "BURDENED"

①

OVERTAKING ③ "B"

OVERTAKEN "P"

RUNNING FREE "B"

④

CLOSE-HAULED "P"

PORT TACK "B"

⑤

STARBOARD TACK "P"

Figure 36. Right of Way

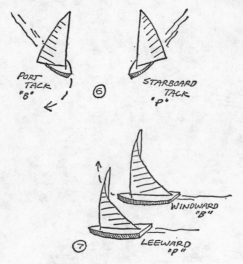

Figure 37. Right of Way

overtaking). (3) Any boat which is being overtaken has the right of way over the boat doing the overtaking. (4) A boat which is CLOSE-HAULED with sails pulled in tight has the right of way over a boat which is RUNNING FREE. (5) If two boats are both close-hauled, the one on the STARBOARD TACK has the right of way over the one on the PORT TACK. (6) Similarly, if two boats are running free, or BEFORE THE WIND, the one with the wind on the starboard side (the sail on the port side) has the right of way. (7) When both boats are on the same tack, either tacking or running free, the boat to LEE-WARD (away from the wind's direction) has the right of way. In spite of rules and their rightness, it should be remembered that not everyone may know them and that being right is less important than avoiding an accident, as a prudent and watchful skipper tries to do. See COLLISION. Mr. O'Day's epitaph puts it thus:

Here lies the body of Michael O'Day
Who died maintaining the right of way.
He was right—dead right—as he sailed along,
But he's just as dead as if he'd been wrong.

Sailboat racing rules differ somewhat from the Rules of the Road. See RACING.

roach Curve along the rear edge (or LEECH) of a three-sided sail. See SAILBOAT PARTS.

road, roads, roadstead Place where ships may ride at anchor, more open than a harbor.

rode Rope attached to the anchor or to the anchor chain of a small boat.

roll To sway from side to side, in contrast to fore-and-aft pitching.

Rolling can be dangerous, as the BOOM can get caught in the water and pull the sail in also (as in BROACHING TO). To moderate rolling, try lowering the CENTERBOARD and pulling in the MAINSAIL a bit. You can also try gently pushing the TILLER back and forth with each wave in such a way as to prevent the rolling. If you have a TOPPING LIFT, pull it up to raise the boom.

roller reef Reef made by rolling the bottom of the sail (FOOT) around the BOOM with a twisting device on the boom. See REEF.

rolling hitch Type of knot.

rope Technically, cord made of fibers or wire twisted together, but the landlubber should remember that a rope becomes a LINE when used in the operation of a sailboat.

Safety and your pocketbook warrant taking good care of your rope. Here are a few hints: (1) Dry wet rope thoroughly before putting it away. (2) Store rope so air can circulate—avoid storage places where air is extremely dry or hot. (3) Avoid dragging rope over rough ground, to prevent chafing and picking up dirt particles that may cut the strands. (4) Keep rope away from paint, cleaning preparations, and other chemicals. (5) Avoid sharp bends and straighten out kinks. (6) When in doubt use a bigger rope—the rule (though a hard one to ascertain and apply) is that a rope's working load should not exceed one-fifth of its stated breaking strength. (7) Reverse your rope periodically to equalize the wear on it; if wear is localized to one section—shift its position. (8) Avoid running large ropes through small SHEAVES—either get larger sheaves or use smaller rope.

rotten stop Lightweight string or thread to tie up a sail temporarily that can be easily broken with a tug to break out the sail.

row To propel a boat with oars along the surface of the water. See Plates 52–55.

rowlock Same as OARLOCK.

rub rail Protective covering on GUNWALE; gunwale guard.

rudder Vertical board which swings at the stern of a boat in the water and which is attached above to a handle, the TILLER, thus enabling the boat to be steered. See Fig. 38.

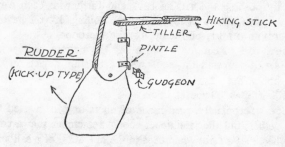

Figure 38. Rudder

The rudder either lies completely under the stern of the boat and is attached to the tiller by a rod coming up through the deck, or (and this is more common in small boats) it is outside and over the back of the boat, the tiller being attached to the top of the rudder in such a way that it extends over (or through) the TRANSOM into the COCKPIT. In this case the rudder is usually detachable by means of pins and eyeholes called PINTLES and GUDGEONS (see Plate 8), or by a TRACK and SLIDE arrangement. Sometimes the lower part can be pivoted up and secured (a KICK-UP RUDDER) for beaching, low tide, or going into shallow waters.

A boat can be steered by its rudder only when it is in motion, because there is then a stream of water flowing past the rudder which pushes it and the stern. The bow then goes in the opposite direction from the stern. Thus when the rudder is pushed to the left, the stern swings right and boat heads left. And one more thing: at times your boat may be in motion in the opposite direction—or *backwards*. In this case, the rudder will also do just the opposite—so, to make the bow of the boat go to the right, put the rudder to the left (and the tiller to the right).

If the rudder (or tiller) breaks or gets lost, you can substitute a paddle, oar, floorboard, or even a whisker pole.

rules of the road Regulations governing water traffic; pilot rules.

Although there are several official sets of rules of the road for different bodies of water (such as International, Inland, Great Lakes, and Western River Rules), in general their application to small sailboats is not great. However, right-of-way rules should be known by sailors, especially with the greatly increasing number of families taking to the water each year. See RIGHT OF WAY.

run 1. Rear (AFT) underwater part of the boat. 2. Sailing course with the wind at one's back and the sails and BOOM let out at right angles to the boat. 3. To sail on such a course, in the direction of the wind, with the wind behind; to run before the wind; to run free; to sail downwind or downhill; to sail off the wind; to scud. See Plate 25.

Of the three positions of sailing—with the wind in front (BEATING), to the side (REACHING), and behind (RUNNING)—the last is usually thought of as the easiest. (See POINTS OF SAILING.) Ostensibly your boat is just blown along like a leaf on the surface of the water, and that's that.

Actually, there is probably more potential danger in *running before the wind* than in beating or reaching (for instance, in an uncontrolled or accidental JIBE). But since it is the least "tippy" of the three and the most roomy, with the sail and boom well out of the way, it can also be considered the pleasantest.

With the wind directly behind you (dead astern), the MAINSAIL is let all the way out (on one side or the other —it does not matter which) by its rope (the MAINSHEET) until it is at right angles to the boat—or just barely touching the SHROUDS. The boom is not quite at a right angle to the boat since the top part of the sail is always a bit more forward than the boom. Because the wind and the boat are both going in the same direction, the CENTERBOARD is not needed to prevent SIDESLIPPING and can be pulled up. (Exceptions are if you are a beginner, or if your boat is unsteady and rolling.) The crew should sit toward the stern to balance the wind on the sail. Otherwise the bow may nose under, or the stern ride up so high out of the water that the RUDDER loses its effectiveness. Be sure your RUNNING BACKSTAYS are tight, if you have them.

The jib. The JIB hangs limply, blanketed by the mainsail, as no wind can reach it. Don't bother about this at first, until you have learned to tell whether or not you might be in danger of an unintentional jibe. The jib's sudden appearance on the other side of the mast will be your warning signal. See JIBE.

But it won't be long before you will want to make purposeful use of the jib to give you more sail area. Pull it out from behind the mainsail and hold it out on the other side of the mast. Your boat is now WUNG-OUT or sailing WING AND WING. See Fig. 39. This is most often done with a WHISKER POLE (though a BOAT HOOK propped against the COAMING is a good substitute). One end of the whisker pole fits against the mast, and the other through the eyehole (CRINGLE) in the outside corner (CLEW) of the jib. The jib SHEET on that side is pulled tight and cleated to help keep the whisker pole in place. Sometimes, especially when racing and on larger boats, a SPINNAKER takes the place of the jib on the DOWNWIND LEG. See SPINNAKER.

Unintentional jibe. Now what about the danger of an unintentional or accidental jibe? We have said that the wind is from your back, but actually this is not 100 per cent true much of the time. It is hard to keep the wind exactly behind you, at 180° from your bow all the time, so what happens when it is a bit to one side or the other? Usually—and this is as it should be—the wind is a bit more on the WINDWARD side, over the back corner of the boat opposite the sail. What you want to avoid is the opposite: letting the wind get on the same side of the boat as the sail (sailing BY THE LEE), since inevitably the wind gets around behind the sail and pushes it to the other side. See Fig. 39. Wind and sail cannot both be

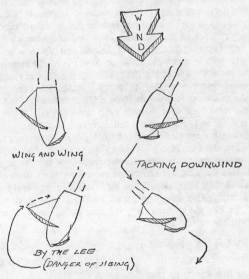

Figure 39. Running

on the same side of the boat at once, so something has got to give, and that something may be your head! Here the TELLTALES come in especially handy, so be sure to have them on your shrouds.

Just as the wind goes from one side of the sail to the other—*via the bow*—when you turn the bow toward the wind and COME ABOUT, so the wind goes from one side of the sail to the other—*via the stern*—when you turn the stern toward the wind (and the bow away from it) and thus jibe. The wind crosses the bow in coming about, the stern in jibing. But notice the difference: as the boat turns *into* the wind in coming about, it loses some momentum as the wind is spilled from the sail; the leading edge of the sail attached to the mast does not have far to go and flutters over gradually (if noisily); whereas in an accidental jibe, the wind suddenly catches the unattached outer edge of the sail (the LEECH), which is way out over the water, and whips it and the boom over to the other side, sometimes with real violence. Injury to equipment and people may result, as well as capsizing.

To avoid jibing accidentally, learn to keep a sharp eye out for the direction and shifts of the wind. If you are not sailing WUNG-OUT, the jib can warn you; or if you feel a lessening of the pressure on the mainsheet, you will know the wind is no longer pushing on the front of the sail; and of course watching your telltale or FLY will show you when the wind has crept over to the sail's side of the boat. When you notice any or all of these things beginning to happen, push the tiller toward the sail, so as to point the boat a bit to windward, and bring the wind back over the side away from the sail. If the wind is shifty and squally, better sail on a very broad reach anyway (or tack downwind) to avoid trouble. See JIBE, TACK, DOWN-WIND and Fig. 39.

Broaching to. Two other dangers to watch out for in going before the wind are BROACHING TO and ROLLING. Both can be avoided by being alert. Since the boom may get caught in the water in either case, you can try hauling it in a bit, or pulling it up with the TOPPING LIFT, and also letting down the centerboard to steady the boat.

run by the lee See BY THE LEE.

run free To sail with the wind behind the boat, to sail before the wind; to run. See RUN.

runner, running backstay Adjustable rope or wire supporting the mast, especially when running before the wind; a backstay.

Runners must be taken care of each time the sail crosses the boat, the one on the same side as the sail (the LEEWARD runner) being let loose, and the opposite one (the WINDWARD runner) being fastened tight as the sail comes over.

running lights Lights on a moving boat.

running rigging Ropes and lines (rigging) which are movable and are pulled up and down, in or out (such as HALYARDS and SHEETS), as opposed to STANDING RIGGING which is not pulled or moved.

S

safety Safety afloat is of prime importance, both to you and the other fellow. Here are some basic safety rules:

(1) Know how to swim.

(2) Let someone on shore know when you are out in your boat and where you plan to go and when you plan to return.

(3) Provide a life jacket or its equivalent for every person aboard the boat.

(4) Take a REEF if needed.

(5) Do not go out if the weather looks bad.

(6) Equip your boat with an oar (or paddle), extra line, a bailer, and a knife.

(7) Stay with your boat if you capsize.

(8) Know the RIGHT OF WAY rules and the meanings of BUOYS.

(9) Do not overload your boat.

(10) Never CLEAT the MAINSHEET.

sail **1.** What this book hopes to help you to do. **2.** Short jaunt in a sailboat. **3.** Piece of cloth, now more often than not synthetic, that enables the wind to propel your boat.

The everyday sails—working sails—of a FORE-AND-AFT-rigged boat, are the MAINSAIL and JIB, to which may be added for speedier sailing the LIGHT SAILS—SPINNAKER, GENOA JIB, and REACHING JIB.

The mainsail, the only sail on a CATBOAT, is usually a three-sided or MARCONI sail, although there are also many four-sided (GAFF-RIG) sails still afloat. The jib is the smaller sail in front of the mast on a SLOOP-rigged boat.

The light sails are used instead of the jib, and are large, light in weight, and more complicated to handle than the smaller jib. See GAFF, MARCONI, READYING, SAILBOAT PARTS, SPINNAKER, SYNTHETICS.

sailboat parts All sailboats have a HULL, RUDDER, RIGGING, SPARS and SAILS.

The nautical vocabulary for all the parts within these five categories is immense. The diagrams illustrate the most common parts. Those listed below are explained in the body of the book, each under its alphabetical listing.

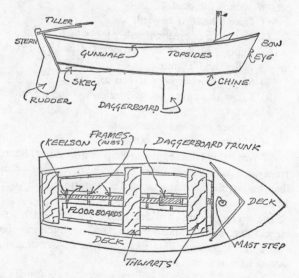

Figure 40. Sailboat Parts—Hull

HULL (See Figs. 15, 40)

ballast
bilge
bitt
bow
centerboard
centerboard trunk
chain plate
chine
chock
cleat
coaming
cockpit
daggerboard
daggerboard trunk
deck
eye
fairlead
fender
floorboards
frame
freeboard
gunwale
helm
keel
keelson
leeboard
limber holes
partner
rail
rib
scupper
sheer
skeg
splashboard
stanchion
stem
step
stern
strake
stringer
taffrail
thwart
tiller
topside
transom
wheel

RUDDER (See Fig. 38)

gudgeon
hiking stick
kick-up rudder
pintle
tiller
tiller extension
yoke

RIGGING (See Figs. 12, 41, 43, 46)

backstay
bight
block
boom vang
bridle
downhaul
earing
eye
fake
fly
forestay
guy
halyard
hawser
headstay
jib halyard
jib sheet
jibstay
knot
lanyard
leech line
line

175

main halyard	shroud
mainsheet	snap hook
marline	snatch block
outhaul	spreader
painter	standing rigging
peak halyard	stay
pennant	stop
pulley	tang
rattail	tackle
runner	telltale
running rigging	throat halyard
shackle	topping lift
sheave	traveler
sheet	turnbuckle

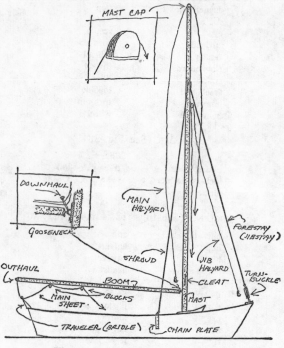

Figure 41. Sailboat Parts—Rigging

SPAR (See Figs. 12, 13, 27, 41)

boom	mizzen
club	peak
gaff	rake
gooseneck	sail track
groove	spinnaker pole
heel	throat
jaw	truck
jigger	whisker pole
mast	yardarm
masthead	

SAIL (See Figs. 34, 42, 44)

balloon jib	cringle
batten	foot
boltrope	genoa
bunt	grommet
clew	head

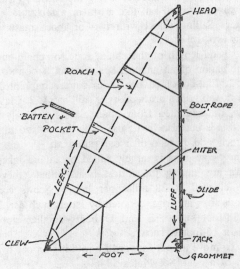

Figure 42. Sailboat Parts—Sail

headboard	pocket
headsail	reaching jib
jib	reef
leech	reef band
luff	reef point
mainsail	roach
miter	slide
mizzen	spinnaker
parachute	tack
peak	throat

sail track   T-shaped metal strip running the length of the mast or BOOM onto which the sail is fitted by means of the lugs or SLIDES sewn along its edge. See Plate 11.

This track-and-slide method of attaching sails to SPARS is one of the two most common methods, the other being by means of a GROOVE. See MAST.

scandalize   To make the area of certain sails smaller (usually in case of a storm) by: (1) Dropping the PEAK, on a GAFF-RIGGED sail. (2) Tying the corners (TACK and CLEW) on a small sail like a JIB or a MIZZEN.

schooner   Sailing vessel with two or more masts and a FORE-AND-AFT RIG.

scope   Total length of the chain, rope, or chain-and-rope combination of an anchor. See ANCHOR, MOORING.

scow   1. Flat-bottomed boat with square unpointed ends (the BOARD BOATS are *scow-type* sailboats). 2. Class boat Scow, differentiated from other classes not only by its blunt ends but also by its use of two BILGE BOARDS, one on each side, instead of a CENTERBOARD.

The Scow class is largely sailed on inland lakes, and Scows are among the fastest boats afloat (they have been clocked at 28 miles per hour). Scows come in various sizes and rigs, denoted by letter, such as: A boat —a 38-foot SLOOP; E and D boats—smaller sloops; C boat—a 16-foot CATBOAT.

scull   To move a boat forward by rotating an oar over the stern of a boat. See Plates 58–60.

Sculling is a dying art that should be rejuvenated,

since it is a very efficient way to propel a small sailboat in case of need.

scupper Drain hole along the edge of the deck (usually used in plural).

sea Disturbance on surface of the water; rough water; waves.

sea anchor Drag put over the side to keep a boat headed into the wind in heavy weather; a DROGUE.

sea buoy Last BUOY as a boat leaves the channel going out to sea.

seam Space between planks on the HULL of a boat.

seaway 1. Place where moderate or rough water is to be found. 2. Channel or ocean traffic lane.

secure To fasten, to make fast.

seize To bind together with SPUN YARN or MARLINE, as *to seize two ropes*.

seizing 1. Act of binding two ropes together. 2. Small rope, yarn, or wire used to lash two ropes.

semaphore alphabet A form of visual signaling by which a message is spelled out with a pair of flags.

serve To cover (a rope or the end of a rope) with SMALL STUFF or MARLINE to protect it.

set 1. To lay out or prescribe, as to *set a course* on which to sail. 2. To hoist and spread to the wind, as to *set the sails*. 3. Direction of tide, current, or wind. 4. Manner in which a sail is pulled up and fastened to its SPARS; shape.

set up To tighten or make taut the last few inches of a HALYARD when raising the sail; to sweat up; to sway up.

shackle Fastening device, as on the end of a HALYARD, to engage the sail.

The most common type of shackle is a U-shaped piece of metal with a pin or bolt across the open end. This pin is removed either by being unscrewed, or pushed back on a spring, so that it can be slipped through the hole in the top (HEAD) of the sail. If the pin is removable, tie it to the shackle as losing it can be disastrous.

179

Other types of shackles use cotter pins, leather thongs, etc., as fastening devices. See Fig. 43.

shank Long part of an anchor; at one end are the CROWN, arms, and points (FLUKES) which dig into the ocean bottom, and at the other end the crosspiece or STOCK to which the rope is attached.

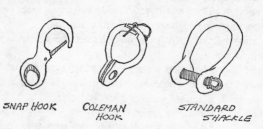

SNAP HOOK   COLEMAN   STANDARD
                    HOOK   SHACKLE

Figure 43. Shackles and Snap Hook

she Correct nautical pronoun to use when referring to a boat (but not used in this book in the interests of simplicity).

sheave (pronounced "shiv") Grooved wheel, or pulley set in a BLOCK or SPAR, often at the top of the mast and at the end of a BOOM. See BLOCK, SAILBOAT PARTS.

sheepshank Type of knot.

sheer Curve of the deck or GUNWALE viewed from the side.

sheet 1. Rope (LINE) by which a sail is let out and pulled in, and thus regulated in relation to the wind. See JIB-SHEET, MAINSHEET, SAILBOAT PARTS.

Never call a sail a sheet, nor a sheet a sheet rope. 2. To be pulled in by a sheet, as a sail is *sheeted in.*

sheet bend Type of knot.

ship 1. Large seagoing vessel, in contrast to a small open craft that is not capable of ocean travel. 2. To have water come in over the side of the boat.

When BEATING, a strong wind or squall can cause the boat to tip so much (HEEL) that water pours into the

COCKPIT and the boat ships water. See HEEL. **3.** To put things in place.

To ship the oars is to bring the oars inside the boat rather than to leave them sticking out over the sides. Always ship your oars when you leave your DINGHY.

shipshape Neat, everything in its place, in good order.

Keeping a boat shipshape is not being finicky. Neatness is functional and essential for safety both under way and when you leave your boat. After sailing, don't be in such a rush to get home to supper that you leave things messy. A storm may come up and blow away or break your GEAR, pull the boat loose, or capsize it.

The steps in leaving a moored boat shipshape include:

(1) Taking down the sails. The JIB should come down practically simultaneously with landing at your MOORING or dock (if not before). Take care not to let it fall overboard or get soiled by the mooring rope on the deck. Lift the coiled jib HALYARD off the CLEAT and lay it end down on the deck so that it will run up freely as the sail comes down. See Plate 49. Undo the sail's SNAP HOOKS from the JIBSTAY and the halyard from the HEAD of the sail as it comes down and secure both ends of the halyard (on the cleat or the bow SHACKLE—each skipper has his own pet method). Now the MAINSAIL: Pull the BOOM into the center of the boat (AMIDSHIPS) so that as the sail comes down it will not fall in the water. Lift off the coil and uncleat the halyard, as on the jib, later also securing both ends. If the sail does not seem to come down readily (the SLIDES may need greasing), pull on the rope in the sail's edge (the BOLTROPE), not the sail itself. Undo the OUTHAUL on the boom and slide the sail forward. Take out and put away the BATTENS (in a safe, dry place on the boat if possible). If the battens are not removable, grasp them all parallel to each other and wrap the sail neatly around them so they will not get broken or poke holes in the sail in storage. Stow the sails in the sail bag, jib last. (If they are wet, do not

181

forget to take them out and dry them when you get home, especially if they are cotton sails.)

(2) Next, be sure all lines are pulled in and coiled, well fastened (but not too tight so as to allow for shrinkage if they are non-synthetic).

(3) Secure the boom. In most boats it is placed on a BOOM CRUTCH near the stern; it can also be lashed down with a rope. Whatever your method, be sure it will not come loose or get battered or lost.

(4) Pull up the CENTERBOARD and secure it by both its pin and PENNANT.

(5) Unfasten the RUDDER and TILLER and lay them carefully in the boat, preferably on something soft so as not to mar the finish. If they are not removable, lash the tiller amidships with the MAINSHEET.

(6) Bail or sponge any water out of the boat. See Plates 56–57.

(7) Collect all your gear.

(8) Put on the canvas COCKPIT COVER, if you have one.

(9) Untie the DINGHY and head for home, secure in the knowledge that your boat is ready for anything.

shoal Shallow water.

shock cord Elastic rope, handy on a boat.

Its speedy fastening and unfastening can be useful for all sorts of things: holding a coil of rope, preventing SHROUDS and HALYARDS from rattling and SLATTING, holding up the SPINNAKER POLE, or FURLING a sail.

shoot 1. To move forward with sails LUFFING on the momentum left after the wind has been spilled out of the sails when heading into the wind, especially in coming up to a MOORING (or a dock); to carry way. 2. Forward momentum or coasting of a boat when headed into the wind; way.

In order to make a successful landing, you should know how much shoot your boat has. A lightweight

CENTERBOARD boat has less shoot than a heavier KEEL boat. Your boat will have less shoot in a light wind than in a strong wind. See LANDING.

shore Place for your sailboat to land on or take off from, in case you may wish to have a swim or a picnic, or in an emergency. See Plates 43, 44.

Beaching your sailboat once in a while will not hurt it. This is an advantage of a small CENTERBOARD sailboat over a larger KEEL boat.

Landing on a beach gives you no choice as to how you will turn into the wind to stop your boat as you do at a float. See LANDING. So try to come in slowly either by letting your SHEETS run out so that the sails spill their wind, or by letting down the sails entirely. Lift your centerboard little by little as it scrapes the bottom. When the RUDDER hits bottom too, stop sailing, remove or pivot up the rudder, and paddle the rest of the way. Do this anyway if you are unsure of the bottom—you do not want to hit a hidden rock going full sail ahead.

With a strong onshore wind another procedure is to head up into the wind as you approach the shore. Drop sails and anchor. Then drift astern onto the beach, slowly PAYING OUT the anchor line.

Tie up to a tree on shore or use your anchor. If you are a saltwater sailor, don't forget to make allowance for the tide. If you go into the interior to picnic, you may return either to find your boat so far up on the shore you will have to spend the night, or on the other hand, several yards out on the billowing waves, perhaps necessitating an unwanted swim.

Leaving from the shore involves getting the boat far enough out so that you can let down the centerboard. If the wind is blowing away from the shore, hoist your sails, have your crew give the boat a good push backward as they jump into it, then BACKWIND the JIB, turn the boat around, pull in your sails, and let down the centerboard. If the wind is blowing against the shore, paddle out a little distance, point the boat into the wind, let down the centerboard, and then pull up your sails. If you are anchored, the boat can be KEDGED into deeper water.

shroud Wire support going from the upper part of the mast to the sides of the boat, contrasted with a STAY, which supports the mast by leading to the bow or the stern, in a lengthwise direction. Both shrouds and stays are part of the STANDING RIGGING. See SAILBOAT PARTS.

sideslip To slide sideways through the water; make leeway.

signal Any method of sending a message. See DISTRESS SIGNAL, INTERNATIONAL CODE.

signaling Methods of communicating by sight or sound.

There are three main systems used at sea for signaling: (1) The MORSE CODE, consisting of a system of dots and dashes to represent letters, numerals, and signals, by flashing light or sound signal. (2) The INTERNATIONAL CODE, which is a system of variously designed flags to represent letters of the alphabet and numerals as well as specific messages. (3) The SEMAPHORE ALPHABET method, in which a signalman with two identical flags forms the letters of the alphabet (and hence simple words) by different arm positions.

skeg Backward extension of the KEEL, which acts as a support for the RUDDER. See SAILBOAT PARTS.

skiff Small lightweight rowboat or sailboat.

skipper One who gives orders, the captain.

slack Loose, not tight; to make loose.

To *slack away* or *slack off* is to let out or EASE, and is usually said of the ropes (SHEETS) controlling the sails.

slack water Period at high or low tide when water is not in motion.

slat To flap noisily, as idle sails or HALYARDS against a mast.

slide Small metal lug fastened at intervals to the front

184

edge (LUFF) and bottom (FOOT) of the mainsail to attach it to mast and BOOM, and enable the sail to be
pulled up on or along the sail TRACK. See SAILBOAT
PARTS and Plate 11.

sliding gunter See GUNTER.

slip **1.** To let go of or leave, as to slip the MOORING. **2.**
Mooring place at a dock between sets of poles or planks.

slipped ring knot See KNOT.

slippery hitch A type of knot.

sloop Sailboat with one mast and two sails, a MAINSAIL
and a JIB.

The mast is set back somewhat from the bow (as
compared to a CATBOAT) so that the jib may be fastened
(BENT) to the FORESTAY in front of the mast. The mainsail, attached to the back of the mast, is usually triangular in shape (MARCONI-RIGGED). See RIG.

The argument over which is better for a beginner—a
catboat (with one sail) or a sloop (with two sails)—is
one which each individual must resolve for himself according to his own needs and desires. Pro-sloop arguments include the following: since eventually almost all
sailors will want to "graduate" to a sloop, why not learn
to handle the jib from the very start? Once hoisted, this
small sail can be secured and left alone except when
COMING ABOUT, so that a sailor *can* handle by himself a
sloop as well as a catboat. A sloop responds better and
more quickly when coming about, and can sail into the
wind more closely. There is less likelihood of an accidental JIBE, since the jib's appearance on the opposite
side of the boat from the mainsail gives warning that the
wind has come around behind you. It is also argued that
since some sloops sail quite well without their jibs, it is
better to have a boat rigged for a jib so that the sailor
can add it to his boat when he is ready for it.

There are small boats on the market today (the Quad,
the Sprite) which can be rigged either as catboats or as

sloops, by changing the position of the mast and adding a jib. See CATBOAT, MAST.

slot Passage between MAINSAIL and JIB through which wind passes.

This slot effect is an important factor in the TRIM of the sails and the speed of the boat. If the jib is pulled in too tight, it will BACKWIND the wind onto the mainsail and make it lose some of its power. When the jib is trimmed correctly—not too tight, not too loose—it creates a pulling effect on the front of the mainsail, giving it more power than a single sail without such a slot. See Plate 24.

small stuff Small ropes, as MARLINE and SPUN YARN, often tarred.

snap hook Metal device with spring catch to attach one thing to another. See Fig. 43.

Snap hooks are often sewn on the forward edge (LUFF) of the JIB to attach it to the JIBSTAY, or on the sail end of a HALYARD.

snatch block See BLOCK.

snub To check suddenly, as to stop a rope from running out.

sound To measure depth of water.

sounding Measurement of depth of water by a weight on a LINE.

sound signal See DISTRESS SIGNAL.

spar General term for the poles to which the sails are attached and BENT as BOOM, MAST, GAFF, YARD.

spar buoy Vertical floating post. See BUOY.

spill the wind To cause the sail to lose its wind, and to flap (LUFF) by turning the bow into the wind or by releasing the rope (the MAINSHEET) which controls the MAINSAIL so that the wind no longer fills the sail; to luff; to luff up.

spinnaker Large, light, spherical three-sided sail, often brightly colored, usually used in racing instead of the

JIB when going before the wind or on a BROAD REACH to increase speed. See Fig. 44 and Plate 27.

The modern parachute spinnaker (sometimes called a chute) has two identical sides (LEECHES) and is set FLYING—that is, it is fastened only at its three corners, rather than along one edge to a mast, BOOM, or STAY. The SPINNAKER POLE stretches from a device which holds it on the mast to a corner of the spinnaker on the opposite side of the boat from the boom. See Plate 28.

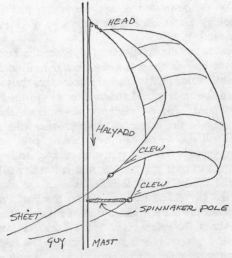

Figure 44. Spinnaker

The top (HEAD) of the spinnaker is pulled up by the spinnaker HALYARD; one lower corner is controlled by the spinnaker SHEET, and the other by the spinnaker GUY; the guy is differentiated from the sheet by the fact that it also controls the spinnaker pole. Since the two lower corners are interchangeable, and the spinnaker pole is changed from one to the other each time it changes sides, first one corner is the TACK, then the other. Technically the corner next to the spinnaker pole is always the tack.

An easy way to keep your spinnaker ready for handy hoisting is in a common cardboard grocery carton. Cut three V-shaped slits in its corners and fold the sail neatly into the box, leaving the three corners of the sail sticking out through the slits. Then the three LINES—the halyard, the sheet, and the guy—can be easily attached to the three corners, ready to raise the spinnaker when you start on the DOWNWIND course. Remember that the lines controlling a spinnaker must always be outside all the other RIGGING.

Now to set the spinnaker: (1) Place the boxed sail near the bow on the side away from the sail and boom (to WINDWARD). (2) Lead the spinnaker halyard out around the JIBSTAY and attach it loosely to the head of the spinnaker. (3) Attach the windward spinnaker rope —the guy—to the corner of the spinnaker (the TACK), which will also be next to the spinnaker pole, and lead the guy outside the windward SHROUD back to its BLOCK or FAIRLEAD near the stern. Secure it loosely. (4) Snap one end of the spinnaker pole—its ends are identical— over the guy a few feet away from the box. Push the other end forward and attach it to its fitting on the mast. (5) Attach the spinnaker TOPPING LIFT (or spinnaker pole lift) which runs from the mast to the middle of the spinnaker pole and supports it there (this is a good place to use SHOCK CORD). (6) Attach the other rope— the spinnaker sheet—to the third corner sticking out of the box (the CLEW), leading it outside the jibstay and the shroud on the LEEWARD side of the boat, under the boom and back toward the stern, and secure. (7) Now, as the boat turns to go before the wind, the halyard is pulled, the spinnaker billows up and out of its box (stow this container away safely for the next time), and the guy and sheet are TRIMMED so that the spinnaker pole and bottom (FOOT) of the spinnaker are parallel to the water. (8) As the guy is trimmed, it pulls the spinnaker as well as the spinnaker pole around on the windward side of the boat; the pole should be approximately at right angles to the mast (and to the direction of the wind). (9) Let down the jib. (10) Keep the spinnaker full and just not LUFFING by playing both guy and sheet; trim the guy so that its edge of the sail does not luff—it will curl and cave in rather than flutter as on the MAIN-SAIL. Give the guy a quick snap as you trim it to remove the curl.

In JIBING the spinnaker, the ends of the spinnaker pole are reversed as it is shifted from one side to the other, and the guy becomes the sheet and the sheet, the guy. First remove the inboard end of the pole from the mast and attach it to the spinnaker sheet near the corner of the spinnaker which has been the clew, so that both ends of the pole are momentarily attached to the two lines at the sail corners. Now, as the boat jibes, detach what has been the outer end of the pole from its old place on the guy at the tack of the spinnaker and fasten that end on the mast. The old guy is now the sheet, and the line which controls the spinnaker boom has become the new guy and should be trimmed as it was on the other side.

In bringing in the spinnaker, be careful not to let it get tangled or fall in the water. First, slacken the guy and push the pole forward so that it is lengthwise to the boat and can be detached from the mast; then release the guy from both pole and sail, and as the halyard is lowered, quickly pull in the spinnaker under the mainsail and over the leeward deck.

It is probably apparent from the above directions, which must be carried out *in addition* to the normal jibing duties, that handling a spinnaker is not for the lone or the beginning skipper. Save it for the day when you have a threesome of experienced salts seeking excitement.

spinnaker boom Same as SPINNAKER POLE.

spinnaker pole SPAR for the large light sail, the SPINNAKER.

Unlike the BOOM (of the MAINSAIL) which is attached all along its edge, the spinnaker pole supports only one corner of the spinnaker. It has identical fittings at each end and is attached by one end to the mast and by the other to the rope (the GUY) at the TACK of the spinnaker. When the boat is JIBED, the ends are reversed. The fitting consists of a closed hook which can be opened or TRIPPED by a spring across the opening, usually on a small line or wire running the length of the pole. See SPINNAKER.

spinnaker pole lift, spinnaker topping lift LINE from mast to middle part of a SPINNAKER POLE to hold it in place; spinnaker lift.

splashboard Board rising up above the deck in front of the mast, usually in a V-shape, to protect passengers and crew from flying spray; a spray rail.

splice Process or result of joining two rope ends together, or making one end into a loop, by braiding strands rather than by tying a knot.

A splice has three advantages over a knot: it permits a rope to pass through the opening of a pulley, or BLOCK, that is too small for a knotted rope; it is neater; and it is stronger. A splice is stronger than a knot because the crossings of its interwoven strands at lesser angles than the crossings of a rope in a knot create less "shearing force."

Since small boats use small ropes, splicing two ropes together is not as economically important to the small boat sailor as an *eye splice*. An eye splice makes a neat, permanent loop on the end of an anchor LINE, HALYARD, or MOORING line and especially around a metal THIMBLE.

Before proceeding through the following steps in making an eye splice, take a piece of rope and examine it. Typically it has three "strands" that are "laid," or twisted. Each strand is made up of several "yarns."

(1) *a*. Unlay, or separate, the strands in the end of a rope for a few inches. How far back to unlay depends on how big the strands are and how long a splice you intend to make—as a rule of thumb, 2–3 turns for non-synthetics, 4–5 turns for synthetics. *b*. Make a counterclockwise loop with the end pointing up, as shown in Fig. 45 (1).

(2) *a*. With your left thumb and forefinger, make an opening in the rope where you want the splice to start by holding one of the three strands apart from the other two strands. *b*. With your right thumb and forefinger, tuck the middle one of the three strand-ends through the opening and pull it up snug. See Fig. 45 (2).

(3) *a*. With your left thumb and forefinger, make another opening by pulling apart the strand to the left of the one you have just released. *b*. With your right thumb and forefinger, tuck the left one of the two remaining strand-ends through the opening and pull it up snug. See Fig. 45 (3).

(4) *a*. With your left thumb and forefinger, make a third opening by pulling apart the strand to the left of the one you have just released. *b*. *Pay special attention to this step—it is the trick to successful splicing.* First, be sure that your loop has revolved so that it is now running in a clockwise direction. See Fig. 45, (4). Then, with your right thumb and forefinger, swing the remaining strand-end *over* the opening, *around* and *through* it, and pull it up snug.

(5) *a*. Still with your right thumb and forefinger holding the strand-end that you tucked in—(4) *b*., above —weave it over and under the adjacent strand of the rope. *b*. Rotate the rope slightly to the right. Pick up the next strand-end and tuck it over and under the adjacent strand of the rope. *c*. Repeat the preceding "over and

191

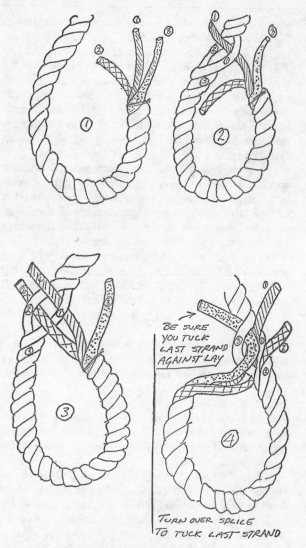

BE SURE YOU TUCK LAST STRAND AGAINST LAY

TURN OVER SPLICE TO TUCK LAST STRAND

Figure 45. Splice

under" process at least two more times. The more tucks, the stronger the splice. For extra neatness, before making the last few tucks, unravel the yarns at the strand-ends and cut away about half of them.

(6) *a.* Roll and pound the splice. *b.* Cut off excess strand-ends.

spray rail Same as SPLASHBOARD.

spreader Horizontal bar on each side of the upper part of the mast which spreads or holds out the wires (SHROUDS) supporting the mast.

spritsail Four-sided sail differing from a GAFF-RIG sail in that the sprit (a pole) extends diagonally from the lower part of the mast across the sail to hold up the outer corner, the PEAK.

spun yarn Coarse yarn, sometimes tarred, for binding ropes or LINES.

squall Sudden gust of wind, likely to make your boat HEEL over.

You can see a squall coming and prepare for it by observing the darker ripples it makes on the water. See HEEL.

square knot See KNOT.

square rig Rig with sails set across the boat rather than lengthwise. See RIG.

stanchion Upright pillar to support guard rails, awnings, etc.

stand by Order to get ready, as *Stand by to raise anchor,* or *Stand by to come about.*

standing part See KNOT.

standing rigging That RIGGING which remains in a fixed position, such as SHROUDS and STAYS, in contrast to RUNNING RIGGING which is pulled up or down, in or out.

starboard Right side of a boat when facing forward; opposite of PORT. See DIRECTION.

starboard tack Sailing with the wind coming from the right side; the sail is on the left or PORT side.

A boat *on the starboard tack,* under practically all

circumstances, has the right of way over a boat on the PORT TACK. See BEAT, RIGHT OF WAY, TACK.

start Slack off; loosen; ease; pay out, said of LINES.

stay Support for the mast, usually of wire; that part of the STANDING RIGGING which runs lengthwise to the bow or stern, in contrast to the SHROUDS which run from the mast to the sides of the boat.

JIBS and STAYSAILS are hoisted on stays. See JIBSTAY, RUNNING BACKSTAY, SAILBOAT PARTS, SHROUD.

stays See MISS STAYS.

staysail Any three-cornered sail attached to a STAY, as the several triangular sails hung between the two masts of a staysail schooner.

stays, in stays See IN IRONS.

steerageway Forward motion sufficient to allow a boat to be steered, to respond to changing the direction of the RUDDER.

stem Foremost piece of wood or other material on a boat, to which its sides and KEEL are fastened.

step 1. Block or frame with a hole into which the mast is placed. 2. To set in place; *to step a mast* is to set it in its erect position.

stern The back (AFT, AFTER) part of a boat; opposite of bow. See SAILBOAT PARTS.

sternway Backward movement, as when caught IN IRONS.

When you are *making sternway*, remember that the action of the TILLER and RUDDER is the reverse of that when you are going forward (making STEERAGEWAY). See RUDDER.

stiff 1. Strong, as of a breeze. 2. Not easily tipped, as of a boat; steady; opposite of TENDER or CRANKY.

stock Crosspiece of an anchor, which is attached in the middle to the long part or SHANK.

stop 1. For directions on how to stop a boat, see LANDING, LUFF. 2. Small rope or piece of canvas used for quick tying and untying, as in holding a sail in place temporarily. 3. Device to hold something temporarily, for instance, the device on the TRACK of the mast to hold the SLIDES in place after they have been put on, prior to hoisting sail.

stopper Short rope, device, or knot to hold something in place temporarily or to check a rope from running. See Plate 20.

storm Bad weather, thundersqualls, hard winds and rains.

On a hot summer's day, if you see a blackening sky and thunderclouds, a storm is coming and you would do well to head for home. First will come the calm before the storm, then the wind, hard and gusty, then the rain, cold and lashing, and then probably calm again and too little wind to get home on. So at the first threatening clouds, if you can't make it back, try to tie up to any possible MOORING place or moored boat; if there is a pebble or sandy beach anywhere near (and yours is a CENTERBOARD boat), run it up there; or anchor if you can with the longest rope possible. Even if your anchor does not reach bottom, it is probably a good idea to leave it in the water, as it may catch sooner or later as you are blown with the storm. Lacking these possibilities, you must ride out the storm. Lower all sails. Lash them and your TILLER securely as well as everything else movable. Have your crew put on life jackets. And if you should go over, *don't* leave the boat. See CAPSIZE, HEAVY WEATHER.

storm canvas, storm sails Set of strong small sails for very windy weather, usually not part of a small boat's GEAR.

storm signals, storm warnings In 1958 a new and simplified system of storm warning displays was adopted, as follows:

    Small craft warning: winds up to 38 mph
      One red pennant (day)
      One red light above one white light (night)
    Gale warning: winds from 39 to 54 mph
      Two red pennants (day)

One white light above one red light (night)

Whole gale warning: winds from 55 to 73 mph

One square red flag with a black square in the center (day)

Two red lights (night)

Hurricane warning: winds 74 mph and above

Two square red flags with black centers (day)

One white light between two red lights displayed vertically (night). See WIND SCALE.

strake Plank running the length of the bottom or side of the HULL.

The *garboard strake* is the lowest plank nearest the KEEL, and the *sheer strake* is the topmost one, the one that follows the SHEER.

strap See EYESTRAP, HIKING STRAP.

stringer Wooden strip running lengthwise to reinforce the FRAME of a HULL.

strut Support or brace.

suit Collection or set of sails needed to sail a boat.

swamp To fill with water.

A CENTERBOARD boat will probably capsize as it swamps. See CAPSIZE. A KEEL boat is a different story, since it does not usually capsize. The danger here when a strong wind or a KNOCKDOWN HEELS the boat way over on its side is from its filling with water and sinking. Your keel boat should therefore be equipped with such non-sink features as air tanks, styrofoam layers, or other buoyancy.

If your boat is swamping so badly that you cannot bail it out as you go, lower the sails and put all the crew to work bailing.

sway up See SWEAT UP.

sweat up To pull up as tight as possible (said of a sail or rope); set up; sway up.

swivel Special link in a chain which allows the chain to turn without kinking. See Fig. 29.

swivel block See BLOCK.

synthetics Chemically produced materials for sails, rope, etc., which are now largely replacing the older cottons and hemps because of their resistance to abrasion, mildew, kinking and swelling when wet, and also because of the ease with which they go through pulleys. (However, for some uses, natural fibers are still superior to synthetics.)

Dacron (or Terelyne) is perhaps at the top of the list in durability as well as in price; the finest sails and LINES are now made of Dacron. It will not stretch and can be stored without drying. Nylon does stretch, but may be used for sails on some small boats, and for SPIN-NAKERS; it is lighter and more closely woven. Nylon lines are also an economical substitute for Dacron on small boats where the amount of stretching is of little consequence. There are still sailors who prefer the feel of cotton sails and lines—but their number is diminishing.

T

tack **1.** Lower front corner of a sail. **2.** Direction of a boat in relation to the wind, as STARBOARD TACK, PORT TACK, or *go on the other tack*. To be on the starboard tack is to be sailing with the wind coming over the right side (starboard) of the boat while the sail is on the left side (port). On the port tack the sail is on the starboard side. **3.** To sail a zigzag course toward the direction from which the wind is coming; to sail to WINDWARD; to beat. **4.** To change the wind from one side of the boat to the other by heading into the wind and causing the BOOM to swing across the boat and the sails to fill on the other side; to come about.

Tacking, in the sense of sailing "against" the wind, as stated in definitions **3** and **4**, means sailing close to the wind (BEATING) in a zigzag direction in order to reach a goal directly in front of you, as well as the actual turning from a "zig" to a "zag" (to go from a port tack to a starboard tack). See BEAT, COME ABOUT.

Most boats cannot sail much closer than at a 45° angle into the wind (why, entails going into the theory of aerodynamics, which is interesting but not necessary for the small boat sailor to know). In order to visualize the direction in which you will be heading when, for example, you change from the port to the starboard tack (come about), look over your shoulder at right angles to your boat. The 45° angle of the port tack plus the 45° angle of the starboard tack means you will swing about 90° when you come about. See Fig. 1.

Long tacks to reach your goal are usually better than

short ones, since they save time and motion. But tides, winds, shallow water, and "traffic" will also influence your decision as to when to change tacks. If you find that your boat does better on one tack than on the other, take advantage of it. Racing involves a whole new set of factors in deciding when to tack, which are not covered in this book.

tack downwind, tack to leeward To go in a zigzag direction before the wind in a series of BROAD REACHES, with the sail first on one side, then on the other, to avoid accidental JIBING, instead of sailing with the wind directly behind you. See RUN.

tackle Combination of ropes and pulleys.

The tackle permits the most convenient location of a rope; it also enables a small force to overcome a larger resistance. Different tackle arrangements may be used to pull the BOOM in or out by the MAINSHEET.

tackle, ground See GROUND TACKLE.

taffrail Rail, usually a handrail, around or across the stern of a boat.

tail 1. Rope SPLICED to a BLOCK with a long end for tying. 2. To move by the stern, as a boat at anchor *tails downstream*.

tang Metal strap used to connect a STAY or SHROUD to the mast.

telltale Device, such as a short piece of yarn or ribbon, tied to the wire (SHROUD) supporting the mast to help the skipper tell the direction of the wind. See WIND.

tender 1. Small boat for ferrying to a larger boat; a dinghy. 2. Easily tipped by the wind; crank; cranky; opposite of STIFF.

thimble Metal concave ring around which a rope or wire loop is fastened to prevent chafing.

throat 1. Upper corner nearest MAST of a four-cornered (GAFF-RIGGED) sail. 2. That end of the upper spar (GAFF) on a four-cornered sail which is next to the mast. See GAFF.

throat halyard Rope by which the sail at the inner end of the GAFF is pulled up. See GAFF.

thwart Crosswise seat in a small boat. See SAILBOAT PARTS.

tide Rise and fall of the ocean, twice each lunar day (every 24 hours, 51 minutes); thus if high tide is at noon, it will be low tide at about 6:00 P.M. and high again shortly after midnight.

Tides vary in height, both from place to place and time to time. Sailors in tidal waters should have a calendar tide table handy. They are usually available from your marine dealer.

The tide (as well as the current) is an important force to be reckoned with, and often bewilders a freshwater sailor the first time he encounters it. It can be both a help and a hindrance. See CURRENT.

Tides are least powerful close to shore, so hug the shore if you are going against the tide; go out into mid-channel if you and the tide are heading in the same direction. (A *foul tide* is one running against you, and a *fair tide* one behind or with you.) If it is coming at you sideways, you must realize that it will carry you in that direction. This can be a help when CLOSE-HAULED: the tide pushing on your LEE bow will counteract the wind pushing on your WINDWARD bow.

Remember to allow for the tide when making a landing: if it is strongly against you, go up closer than you would normally before you head into the wind to stop, as the tide will reduce your SHOOT. Similarly, make allowance for a tide which pushes you from the side as you approach your stopping place.

If you tie up to a dock at high tide, leave enough rope for your boat to drop with the tide, or you will return to find it either "hanging on a line" or gone, because the PAINTER has broken (PARTED).

If you beach your boat at high tide, you must push it out a few feet every little while, or it will be stranded as the tide recedes. Beaching at low tide calls for a long line to a rock, tree, or to your anchor placed above the level of high tide. Without such precautions you will probably have to swim to get on board.

tiller Boat's steering device; the wooden stick or arm connected to the top of the RUDDER by which it is moved; helm.

The tiller is sometimes connected permanently to the rudder so that the two are demountable together; or the tiller alone may be removable from the rudder; or both may be fixed in place.

Always be sure the tiller is attached and in place and untied before you raise the sail; and taken off, put away, or lashed in the center of the boat when you are not sailing.

The helmsman should sit where he does not get in the way of the tiller as it is moved back and forth to steer the boat. Sometimes a TILLER EXTENSION enables him to sit farther away on the deck.

Remember that pushing the tiller in one direction heads the bow of the boat in the opposite direction: if you pull the tiller to the right (STARBOARD), your bow will turn to the left (PORT); if you push the tiller to port, the boat swings to starboard. See RUDDER.

tiller extension Short stick which folds on the TILLER when not in use and which, unfolded at right angles to the tiller, allows the skipper to sit farther out on the high side (to HIKE OUT) when the boat is HEELING; folding tiller; hiking stick. See RUDDER.

toggle Wooden pin tapered at both ends which can be slipped through a loop of rope or chain, and quickly engaged or disengaged.

topping lift Rope or LINE, running from high on the mast to the outer end of a BOOM to hold it in place or to raise it. See Fig. 12.

topside, topsides Sides of the boat between the waterline and the deck; above or on the deck.

tow 1. To pull behind a boat. 2. Act of pulling something, usually another boat.

For extra security the towing line should be extended around the mast of the boat being towed. One person should also sit in it to help steer with the TILLER. See Plate 41.

When towing a DINGHY it may be necessary to adjust the height of the towing line on the STEM of the dinghy, to extend the line, or to put in ballast, such as a tied-down outboard motor, in order to reduce YAWING.

track 1. See SAIL TRACK. 2. Course taken by a boat; the wake.

transom Vertical board at the stern of a small boat to which the sides and bottom are attached.

trailer Frame on wheels to haul a sailboat on land. See Plate 62.

Sailing has become available to thousands more people because of trailers. Launching ramps are increasingly part of public waterfront facilities. Thus the sailor can keep his boat in his backyard and sail wherever he likes without the cost of a MOORING or yacht club. Trailer sailing is one type of DRY SAILING.

A trailer also affords good winter storage for your boat. Jack it up on blocks and secure a waterproof cover over the boat. Sailing your boat away from its trailer launching spot requires the same techniques as leaving a beach. See SHORE.

trapeze Wire and belt device to enable crew to climb out to WINDWARD so as to balance the boat when sailing into the wind (BEATING); a refinement or extension of a HIKING STRAP.

traveler Rod (also wire or rope) running across the stern of a boat for the MAINSHEET; bridle.

The mainsheet runs through a BLOCK which slides back and forth on the traveler each time the sail crosses over, as the boat GOES ABOUT.

A traveler on the deck in front of the mast may also

be used on larger boats for the JIB SHEETS. See MAIN-
SHEET, SAILBOAT PARTS.

triangular course Racing course with three sides (LEGS).
See COURSE.

trim **1.** Neat and shipshape. **2.** Way in which a boat sits
in the water, both lengthwise and crosswise.

It should not tip to WINDWARD or HEEL over so far to
LEEWARD that its RUDDER and CENTERBOARD cannot
function efficiently; its bow should neither nose under
nor yet ride up too high. All these and other factors
affect the trim of your boat. **3.** To adjust a boat's trim.
4. Position of the sails (rather than the whole boat) and
the way in which they are set. **5.** To arrange the sails by
pulling them in or letting them out, according to the relation of the boat to the wind. **6.** To pull in the sail—*trim
in* and *trim* in this case are used interchangeably.

The proper trim of the sails is an important refinement that comes with experience and is hard to pass
along in simple terms, since it involves balance, sight,
sound, touch, feel, etc. Suffice it to say here that the
sails should always be full, but just to the point at which
they are not fluttering (LUFFING). If they are not full
and are allowed to luff, you will lose speed, and if they
are full too far *beyond* the point of luffing, you will be
either going off your course, not taking advantage of the
wind, or putting yourself in possible danger of shipping
water or capsizing.

When you are BEATING and TACKING, the trim of the
sails is pretty constantly all the way in (unless you have
to let them out to meet a puff, and in this case you should
immediately trim them in again); but in REACHING and
RUNNING the sails must be constantly trimmed to take
full advantage of the wind. Follow the rule of letting
out the MAINSAIL until it just begins to flutter; then pull
it in—and repeat from time to time.

The JIB too must be continually trimmed as you

change course. In beating it should be let out to a point where it will not BACKWIND the wind onto the mainsail, but no farther; in reaching, its angle is approximately that of the mainsail.

On the other hand, if you are having difficulty in knowing what to do because you cannot seem to tell just where the wind is coming from, the trim of your sails when full will help you to figure out what you are doing. If your BOOM is somewhat out beyond the side of the boat but not all the way out, you are on a BEAM REACH, and the wind is blowing across the boat from the side opposite the sail. Because the wind is thus crosswise or at right angles to the boat, beam reaching is the one sailing action which can be used to go in two exactly opposite directions, i.e., you can go off in one direction with the wind on your left and the sail on your right and then turn around and come back in the other direction with the wind on your right and the sail on your left. In both cases you will be on a beam reach.

If your sail is all the way out at right angles to the boat, the wind is behind you and you are sailing before the wind, or running. Until you have learned about JIBING, you would probably do well to push the TILLER to leeward and pull in the sail a bit so that you are back on a BROAD REACH and do not run the risk of an accidental jibe.

If you are HEELING the chances are the sail is pulled in as far as possible over the COCKPIT and you are beating, with the wind as close to being ahead of you as it can be. To tip less, let out the sail so that it flaps. Then if you want to go back to your reach, pull the tiller to windward till the sail fills. If you prefer to continue beating, trim in your sail till it is CLOSE-HAULED once more.

Trim thus covers a variety of possibilities, all of which can be put into one basic tenet of sailing: Whenever you push or pull the tiller to change the direction of your boat, you must also pull in or let out your sails.

trip 1. To pull the anchor off the bottom. **2.** To unfasten or release, especially by a spring.

A SPINNAKER pole's hook is tripped by a trip line so that it may be attached to the mast or the spinnaker GUY.

truck Very top of the mast.

true north See COMPASS.

trunk Vertical enclosure encasing a slot through the bottom of the HULL, for the CENTERBOARD or DAGGERBOARD. See SAILBOAT PARTS.

trysail Small rugged MAINSAIL for stormy weather.

tune To make changes or adjustments in the boat, its rigging, fittings, or sails to bring about better performance.

Tuning the mast on small boats is undertaken to make sure it is straight. See MAST. Its FORE-AND-AFT tuning can be done while at anchor, usually by merely tightening or loosening the TURNBUCKLE on the HEADSTAY. You can check the need for sideways tuning when sailing on a BEAT (but head your boat into the wind to make the adjustments). If the mast bends, adjust the SHROUDS—the WINDWARD shroud should be tight and the LEEWARD one slack. Then sail on the other TACK and double check.

Wooden masts that are slightly warped can often be straightened out by tuning.

"Tuning up" the whole boat is a science unto itself—and one for racing sailors, not beginners.

turk's head Ornamental knot, so-called because of its resemblance to a turban.

turn Loop in a rope; *to take a turn* is to loop a rope around something to hold it.

turnbuckle Tightening device made up of a cylindrical hollow piece of metal, threaded right-handed at one end and swiveled or threaded left-handed at the other, so that a wire rope set into it can be shortened by twisting the turnbuckle; usually used on STAYS, STANDING RIGGING. See Fig. 46.

turn turtle To capsize by turning over completely so that the mast is pointing down to the bottom. See Plate 36.

twelve-meter boat See METER CLASS.

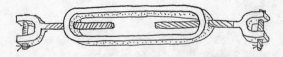

Figure 46. Turnbuckle

U

unbend To remove sails from SPARS and STAYS. See SHIP-SHAPE.

underhand loop See KNOT.

under the lee Protected from the wind—by land, by another boat, or by any object. See LEE.

under way Moving through the water; not tied or anchored.

To get under way is to untie your boat and leave your MOORING or dock. First and foremost, no matter how or where your boat is secured, note the direction of the wind—by the waves, signs on the shore, the FLY at the top of your mast, or the TELLTALES. See WIND.

Getting under way from a mooring. Your boat is pointing with its bow into the wind (unless the current is stronger than the wind), your CENTERBOARD is down, your sails have been hoisted and are flapping, and the ropes (SHEETS) by which you will control the sails are untangled and unfastened. If the harbor is not crowded and you do not have to watch out for boats moored nearby, getting under way is not difficult. Plan to go off on a REACH, with the wind to one side, since that is the best way for a beginner. (1) Untie your DINGHY from the stern of the sailboat where it has been swinging while you were putting on the sail (See READYING THE BOAT), and tie it to your mooring buoy on the side away from the direction you plan to go. (2) Sit on the high (WINDWARD) side of the boat, the opposite side from where the sail will be when it fills, and grasp the TILLER and the LINE (the MAINSHEET) which pulls in and lets out the MAINSAIL. (3) Have your crew go forward and untie but not release the mooring line until you are sure that the centerboard and RUDDER will not get caught in it, that the dinghy is out of the way, and that you are headed where you want to be. A good procedure is to hold onto the mooring line and walk back into the COCKPIT before letting it go (CASTING OFF). This also gives the boat forward motion (WAY). (4) Pull the tiller toward you to head the boat away from the wind and to fill the sail. (5) Pull in (TRIM) the mainsheet so that the sail and BOOM are out over the water at about a 45° angle to the boat. Don't CLEAT the mainsheet. (6) Trim the JIB SHEET (if you have a jib) which is on the same side as the mainsail (the other jib sheet remains free and untouched until you change direction) so that the jib is about parallel to the mainsail, and cleat it. (7) Once under way ease your tiller back to the center of the boat so as not to keep heading away from the wind (FALLING OFF); choose a point to sail for, trim your sail to where it is just not LUFFING, and you're off!

Getting away from a dock or float. Leaving a dock will be much the same as leaving a mooring as long as you are tied up at a three-sided dock where you can hoist sail with your bow heading into the wind and your boat swinging freely away from the dock. With the skipper ready at the tiller, a member of the crew goes forward, pulls the boat up to the dock by its rope (PAINTER) and shoves off sideways with a foot or an arm as he takes the rope inboard. (By contrast, the mooring rope usually stays at the mooring.) Now you are off on your reach.

If the dock is crowded with many boats lined up side by side, raise your sail and then have someone give you a push straight backwards (with the tiller held in the center) until you are clear and can turn the boat in the desired direction and thus get under way. If this seems difficult, ask permission to tie up behind another boat and then shove off from it as from a dock after your sails are hoisted. Or you can even paddle out and raise your sails when you are clear.

If the wind is blowing directly against the dock, one solution is again to push off and paddle out a little distance before pointing the bow into the wind and raising sail. Another possibility for an agile crew in a small boat is to hoist the sail at the dock (be sure you have FENDERS to protect the side of the boat next to the dock) and as the BOOM blows out over the dock, have a member of the crew get onto the dock and push the end of the boom against the mast to make the boat swing out and away toward the wind. He must be quick to jump in again as the sails fill. If an onlooker can be enlisted to do the job, so much the better.

Always remember that near the shore the breezes can be changeable and tricky, now coming from one direction and now from another; now strong, now weak. So watch your wind and try to anticipate it rather than be caught by it.

Sometimes getting under way does not go smoothly. Your sail does not fill after you cast off, the boat will not go forward, and you feel as though you were caught IN IRONS. You may even start to drift backward. For what to do if you are having this difficulty, see IN IRONS.

unship To remove something from its proper place.

up Toward the direction of the wind.

To head up is to point the boat toward the wind. (However, *to put the helm up* means to bring the tiller up to the high—or WINDWARD—side of the boat; this has the effect of turning the boat *away* from the wind.) See DIRECTION, HELM.

uphill Toward the wind; to windward.

upwind Toward the direction from which the wind is blowing; a boat *moves upwind* by BEATING and TACKING.

U. S. Coast Guard Arm of the U. S. Government responsible for all types of aid to boats in coastal waters, as well as for customs and immigration inspection.

Founded at the suggestion of Alexander Hamilton in 1790, the Coast Guard patrols many thousands of miles, carrying out its charge of care and protection of people and craft on the water, as well as maintaining the many NAVIGATIONAL AIDS, such as lighthouses, lightships, BUOYS, etc.

U. S. Coast Guard Auxiliary A volunteer organization, officially authorized by Congress to assist the Coast Guard in promoting safety on water; it provides training in seamanship, training materials, inspection of private boats on request, and other services.

U. S. Power Squadron A non-profit, non-governmental educational organization founded in 1912 to stimulate interest in and develop knowledge concerning boats and to cooperate with governmental agencies.

Its classes are given all over the United States and cover the essentials of small boat navigation under both power and sail. Anyone may take the courses, which are free, but only adult males can join the Power Squadron. For full information write the U. S. Power Squadron, P. O. Box 510, Englewood, New Jersey.

V

variation Difference in compass reading due to difference between *magnetic* and *true North Pole*. See COMPASS.

v-bottom Type of hull shaped like a V. See HULL.

veer To change direction, said of the wind (usually in a clockwise direction); to change a boat's course by turning away from the wind. See HAUL.

W

wake Track on the water behind a boat.

The wake of your boat can help you to determine whether or not you are slipping sideways. If it is straight behind you, fine. If it slants away from you, so that you can see you are dropping to LEEWARD, try letting down your CENTERBOARD farther.

warp **1.** To move a boat by pulling on ropes fastened to a dock. **2.** Rope used for warping.

wash Waves from a boat.

way Progress or motion.

To gather way is to begin to move forward as the wind fills the sails. HEADWAY or STEERAGEWAY is forward motion, STERNWAY is backward motion; LEEWAY is motion to the side. See UNDER WAY.

wear To JIBE, especially from a REACH or a TACK.

weather **1.** To come through safely, as to *weather a storm.* **2.** To pass to the WINDWARD of. **3.** Toward the direction from which the wind is blowing; thus the *weather side* of the boat is the one which the wind strikes first, whereas the LEE side is the opposite one; windward; opposite of lee or LEEWARD.

weather helm Tendency of the boat to turn toward or into the wind and the TILLER to go to the LEE side, so that the helmsman must keep pulling the tiller to the WINDWARD (or WEATHER) side of the boat.

If the tiller is left untouched and the sails UNTRIMMED, the boat will turn toward the wind by itself. The opposite tendency, when the boat heads away from the wind, is a LEE HELM. Test your boat by releasing the tiller and SHEETS and see which way the bow turns.

Sailboats *should* have a slight weather helm so that in case of any sort of emergency the boat will automatically head up into the wind and LUFF. On the other hand, too strong a weather helm can become very tiring if it is continually necessary to pull the tiller hard to windward to keep the boat on its course. This tendency is unavoidable in strong winds.

A lee helm is dangerous. If the tiller should be left unattended, a squall could knock you over or cause other damage. Even if the tiller is under control, a lee helm means that you must continually push the tiller to leeward to spill the puffs of wind or just to stay on your course, and this can be not only awkward but also dangerous in a stiff wind.

Remedies for counteracting a weather or lee helm can best be understood if you think of your boat as turning on a vertical pivot or axis through its center, like a child's propeller blade with a pin in the middle of it. If the propeller is perfectly balanced, a force hitting it pushes both ends equally. But unbalance it, move the axis or pin forward so that the back part is longer, and the wind immediately pushes this longer end away, and the shorter front part turns toward the wind. Now move the pivot backward and the longer part in the front is the one to be pushed away from the wind. Weight added to the short back end would also accentuate the movement away from the wind of the lighter forward part.

A lee helm is analogous to the axis and weight being too far back: to correct it, therefore, the force of the wind against the front part of the boat must be somehow reduced or the force on the back increased, and the weight in the back moved forward or reduced. So, to correct a lee helm, try one or more of these various temporary or permanent measures: (1) Reduce the JIB's pulling power—let it luff or make it smaller. (2) In-

216

crease the MAINSAIL's pulling power—keep it full, or tilt (RAKE) the mast backward (by loosening the FORESTAY and tightening the BACKSTAY). (3) Move the CENTER-BOARD forward or let it down all the way. (4) Move your BALLAST (crew) forward. (5) Restep the mast so that it is farther back (AFT).

If there is too strong a weather helm, the opposite measures are applicable—and remember particularly the temporary ones when the wind is strong and your arm is getting tired: (1) Increase the jib's pulling power or size—be sure it is trimmed in well. (2) Decrease the mainsail's pulling power—by taking a REEF or letting it luff, or by raking the mast forward. (3) Move the centerboard backward (AFT), or raise it a little. (4) Move your ballast toward the stern. (5) Restep the mast farther forward.

wheel Steering device on larger boats.

A small boat skipper who becomes used to the TILLER which is pushed to the right to make the boat go to the left, must remember that both wheel and boat turn in the same direction, as on an automobile.

whip To bind the end of a rope with yarn or cord to prevent the strands from fraying or unravelling (see Fig. 47); back splicing or tucking the strand-ends back into the rope accomplishes the same purpose.

Tape often takes the place of whipping nowadays, especially on a temporary basis. On synthetic LINES, the

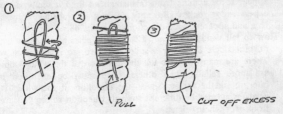

Figure 47. Whip

217

ends are seared with a match, candle or hot knife to fuse the strands and prevent COW'S-TAILS.

whisker pole Light pole used to prop out the JIB on the opposite side from the MAINSAIL in the WING AND WING position when RUNNING before the wind.

One end is inserted in the CLEW of the jib, the other is usually supported against the mast, either by a hook or by JAWS. See RUN.

whistle buoy Warning buoy for ships at sea which whistles from the action of the waves.

whitecap White crest of a wave breaking, denoting a stiff breeze.

winch Device to facilitate hauling in ropes.

wind The force that makes a sailboat go.

Sailors refer to the direction of the wind by the compass direction *from* which it is blowing, not *toward* which it is going. Thus a wind coming from the west, going toward the east, is a west wind. On sailing diagrams the wind direction is indicated by an arrow. The direction of the tail of the arrow denotes the wind direction. Thus in Fig. 49 the arrow indicates an east wind.

Apparent and true wind. Wind directions are referred to as either "apparent" or "true." True wind direction is given by a wind indicator on a *stationary* object, e.g., a flag on a flagpole, a wind sock, smoke from a chimney, etc.

On *moving* objects, however, wind indicators such as PENNANTS and TELLTALES on boats indicate only an apparent wind direction. The forward motion of the boat causes a wind indicator to swing slightly sternwards. This makes the wind appear to be coming from farther ahead than it really is. An expert sailor makes allowance for the discrepancy between true and apparent wind directions. See Fig. 48.

How to tell wind direction. This skill is perhaps the most important single thing for a sailor to learn, so master it now. There are many ways to tell the direction of the wind—some are more reliable than others. Care must be exercised in interpreting the various signs—the direction of the wind 100 yards away may be different from its direction where you are. Look for these signs:

(1) Signs on the land. See Fig. 49. *a*. The branches and

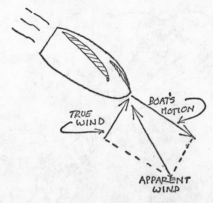

Figure 48. Apparent and True Wind

leaves of trees blowing in the wind. *b.* Smoke from factory chimneys or fires. *c.* Flags and weather vanes on houses, yacht clubs, etc.

(2) Signs on the water. See Fig. 49. *a.* Motion of the surface water—not necessarily the waves, for sometimes there is a discrepancy between the direction of the wind and waves, especially if a swell has built up or the wind has suddenly shifted. *b.* Catspaws and squalls—watch for the little ripples formed on a calm surface by an approaching breeze, or the dark patches made by squalls on top of the existing heavy weather waves. *c.* Boats at their moorings—these boats swing away from the wind with their bows pointing in the wind's direction. (But beware of this sign where the tide or current may also be swinging the boat.)

(3) Signs on the boat. *a.* Telltales—a telltale (also called a FLY or HAWK) indicates apparent wind direction on a moving boat. *b.* LUFF of the sail—when your boat is pointed so that the sails are empty of wind and flapping and the BOOM is in the center of the boat, you are heading directly toward the direction the wind is blowing from. (Then you know that when you fill the sails and get under way CLOSE-HAULED, you will be sailing about 45° away from this direction, since this is as close as most sailboats can sail into the wind.) *c.* Finger, cheek, etc.—a wet finger or cheek feels cooler on the side nearest the wind. You can also feel your hair being blown on

219

SMOKE

WIND

FLAGS

TREES

DIRECTION OF
BOAT AT
MOORING

"CATSPAWS"

WIND DIRECTION

45° APPROX.

TELLTALE

N
W E
S

Figure 49. Wind

the side next to the wind. Cigarette smoke is a valuable guide in light airs.

windlass Drum or barrel with a crank to facilitate hauling in a rope.

wind scale Admiral Sir Francis Beaufort's 1805 wind scale with subsequent modifications.

The wind scale is the standard guide for measuring and describing wind and water conditions. Check this table when you hear the weather reports over the radio to know what sort of sailing to expect.

windward Toward the direction from which the wind blows; on that side of a boat (or an object) which the wind strikes first; on the opposite side of the boat from the sail; toward the wind; weather; the opposite of LEE-WARD; also the side itself nearest the wind, as in the phrase *sit to windward*.

Windward is "up" (and leeward is "down") as a boat normally tips (HEELS) a bit toward the side the sail is on. The skipper should sit to windward whenever possible.

Sailing to windward means BEATING or TACKING. See BEAT, DIRECTION.

wing and wing Sailing before the wind with the JIB held out by a WHISKER POLE (or other artificial means such as a BOAT HOOK, or an arm) on the opposite side of the mast from the MAINSAIL. In this way use is made of the jib's sail area which would otherwise be hanging slack behind the mainsail. See RUN and Plate 26.

work, work to windward, work up To beat; to tack; to sail on the wind, CLOSE-HAULED.

working sails Regular sails on a boat—the MAINSAIL and JIB—in contrast to LIGHT SAILS, such as the GENOA, SPIN-NAKER, etc. See SAIL.

wung-out Sailing WING AND WING, with JIB on one side and MAINSAIL on the other while going before the wind. See RUN.

BEAUFORT WIND SCALE

Wind Force Beaufort No.	Wind in Knots	Description of Wind	Description of Water	Description of Sailboat
0	Under 1	Calm	Glassy	Becalmed
1	1 – 3	Light air	Catspaws	Just under way
2	4 – 6	Light breeze	Rippled	Sails fill nicely
3	7 – 10	Gentle breeze	Wavelets	Slight heel
4	11 – 16	Moderate breeze	Waves	Good heel
5	17 – 21	Fresh breeze	Some whitecaps	Maximum heel or reefed
6	22 – 27	Strong breeze	Many whitecaps	Wet and pounding (head for home)
7	28 – 33	Moderate gale	Foam flies	Hove to, sails lowered
8	34 – 40	Fresh gale	Wild confusion	
9	41 – 47	Strong gale	" "	
10	48 – 55	Whole gale	" "	
11	56 – 63	Storm	" "	
12	Over 63	Hurricane	" "	

Figure 50. Beaufort Wind Scale

Y

yacht Privately owned pleasure boat.

Your sailing DINGHY as well as the America's Cup winner may be called a yacht.

yacht ensign See ENSIGN.

yard Pole (SPAR) hoisted up the mast, from which square sails (or nowadays, LATEEN and LUG sails), flags, or lights are hung.

yardarm Tapering end of a yard.

yaw To have difficulty in keeping on a course, usually because of wind and waves.

A DINGHY being towed may yaw, but less so if it has an upturned bow and one or more KEELS on the bottom. See TOW.

yawl Two-masted boat with smaller mast set back of the TILLER. See RIG.

yoke Piece across the top of a RUDDER with which to control it.

Ropes may be attached to either side of the yoke and led forward into the boat to be used instead of a TILLER, as on the rudder of a sailing canoe.

Z

zigzagging Weaving course necessary to reach many sailing destinations; unless you know how to change your course you will end up only where nature's forces take you—which may be on a rock or against another boat.

Zigzagging is a fitting last word, since it symbolizes the justification for this book and the most lasting thought we would like to convey. Learning to sail is lots of fun, but even more important, it teaches some basic principles for a better world. Few of man's goals can be had by just letting nature take its course; man must learn more about how to harness the forces of nature and how to adjust to the pursuits of other people, in short, when and how to zig and zag.

O17

LOG